Christmas 05

Ty & Mic

Text copyright © 2005 by Charles Fergus
Illustrations copyright © 2005 by Rod Crossman

Design by Chilton Creative

ISBN 0-89272-615-6
Library of Congress Control Number: 2005921863

Printed at Versa Press Inc., East Peoria, Illinois

5   4   3   2   1

Countrysport Press
P. O. Box 679
Camden, ME 04843

Countrysport Press is a division of Down East Enterprise,
publishers of *Shooting Sportsman* magazine. For book orders
or catalog information, call 1-800-685-7962,
or visit www.countrysportpress.com.

For Bob, Carl, Dale,
and, as always, for Nancy and Will

It isn't the bag that matters but the places you go to make it . . .
the wild places in the hills leave a mark on a man's soul.
—Patrick McGinley, *Bogmail*

Chapter 1

I click the shotgun shut. The spaniel sits, her tail lashing, her eyes on the still-green stalks of goldenrod, the rank weeds, the tangled blackberry canes and thornapple stems. I speak her name: "Caillie." She does not turn her head. So we wait; on my part, with excitement building, and also with annoyance, which, taking a deep breath, I work to overcome.

"Caillie." Still nothing, so I pip on the whistle, and at this she finally gives me her attention. Her eyes meet mine. Before she can abandon me again, I say "Hunt 'em up!" and, with a wave of my hand, signal to one side. She dashes off in that direction, charging into the brush.

I follow. It's astonishing, how quickly the sense of pure anticipation returns. It builds from my listening intently for the sound of a gamebird's wings. It comes from keeping a soft focus at the edge of my vision, ready to detect sudden motion, while concentrating a predator's hard focus out in front, alert for a hitch in the dog's movements as she takes scent, or for a grouse or a woodcock launching itself from the ground. Anticipation also arises out of the memories of hunts past.

Caillie and I are entering the first covert of the year, and already I can feel myself returning to that welcome state of immersion—in this moment, this place, this hunt.

I have taken only a dozen steps before Caillie is too far out in front: if a bird were to flush just a few feet ahead of her, I would not have a shot at it. I pip on the whistle, a single sharp note. I am pleased to see her "hup"— sit down, in the parlance of those who hunt behind spaniels—even if she does not then turn her head and look at me.

It is tempting to believe that once you have trained a dog, all you need to do is put her down in game cover and she will take up where she left off at last season's end. I know it doesn't work that way, and I know I'll be spending the first few hunts this year conducting schooling that I should have taken care of during the summer. I decide to let Caillie sit for a while and calm down; better yet, she should sit at my feet. I blow a series of staccato pips, and back she comes, reeled in by the whistle. Another single pip, and she hups.

Still not looking in my direction.

I wonder what she thinks of me, this submissive yet willful bitch, who is fast and agile, whose legs are longer and slimmer than any spaniel's need be. What am I? A slow, staring, tottering biped, tyrannical to boot? Sometimes my shotgun provides a bird to retrieve, but not often enough. Does she consider me an impediment to her own hunting? There's a bit of a disconnect here, or perhaps a connection incompletely made. It's a situation that I have lived with for a long time and will continue working to overcome, because I need this dog, and I love her, albeit differently than I loved my first springer, Jenny, dead now for almost a year.

We wait.

Caillie looks searchingly into the brush and continues to pay me little heed. I glance ahead. The covert is shaped like an oversized football field, a long, lopsided rectangle whose far end is just visible from where I stand. This plot of ground is walled in on all four sides by trees: weedy red maples, twisted black locusts, here and there a tall, upright red oak or a shagbark hickory standing like a solid citizen among the rabble. The trees still hold onto their leaves. The maples' leaves are the brightest and the most various: a mixture of reds, oranges, and yellows, overlaid on green. The locusts' filigreed foliage is a wan yellow. Hickory leaves shine a rich yellow, like candle flame, while oak leaves remain a deep, glossy green. The saw-toothed compound leaves of sumacs burn a brilliant orange beneath the shrubs' fuzzy maroon seed bobs. The crabapples' jagged-edged leaves are a dull and mottled greenish yellow. It's hard to believe, but this disheveled, overgrown place was once a farm.

I remember some excellent hunts in this covert. I recall finding it, almost thirty years ago. It was a brilliant late October day. Three of us put an aluminum canoe into Bald Eagle Creek near the elementary school. We scraped through the shallows and paddled through the deadwaters, stopping here and there to check out prospective game coverts—logging cuts, tangles of streamside alders, abandoned fields reverting to brush. Aspens grew in the old fields, and seedling pines, and crabapples scarcely taller than a man's head. I remember shooting at a grouse not far from where I now stand. I had no dog back then to give me advance warning; grouse in their noisy flight tended to startle rather than galvanize me; and I was an untrained wingshot. In those days, when I pulled the trigger it was rare indeed for a fleeing bird to come a cropper and fall out of that vast expanse of air. I can still see the way the grouse seemingly materialized from the open, leaf-scattered ground beneath a crabapple. On thundering wings it dodged upward through the crooked branches, its cream-colored breast flashing against the sky as it banked to cross the creek. Nowadays, I probably would kill that bird at the top of its rise. On that day more than a quarter of a century ago, I got off two tardy, futile shots—then consoled myself with the fact that at least I hadn't stood there gawking. Observing the bird's line of flight, I'd watched it vanish into more good-looking cover on the creek's opposite bank.

I went back later that year, parking along the highway and following a deer trail down to the creek. I was surprised at how close to the road those twin pockets of brush really were. I decided to call the place Everyman's Covert, since it was so easy to get to, and added it to my list of spots in which to hunt. Over the years I found and shot a good number of grouse and woodcock there, mainly grouse on the higher, drier south bank, and woodcock on both sides of the creek but more often in the low flats on the

A HUNTER'S BOOK OF DAYS

9

north side. Belying the name I'd given it, I remember meeting only one other hunter in Everyman's Covert.

After I got Jenny, she and I usually hunted there three or four times each season. One day in particular comes to mind. It was in late November. Heavy wet flakes of snow fell straight down. The snow coated the pines and stripped off the last of the deciduous trees' leaves. Slushy snow soaks through leather boots like no other substance, and when we'd finished hunting the "grouse side" of the creek my feet were so wet I simply waded through the knee-deep water to the "woodcock side." On the far bank, I tossed aside the stick I'd used to brace myself while crossing. I hupped Jenny, and she sat, her tail slapping against the snow, looking at me with that intense, enthusiastic expression that seemed to say, "All right, what's next?" I cast her off into the catclaw briars and blackberry canes. Jenny was, by then, a seasoned bird dog. She had the power to run hard and quarter the ground thoroughly in the thinner cover of pheasant fields, tempered by the wisdom to slow down and beat the brush in the thicker places where grouse and woodcock dwell. She was soaked to the skin after swimming the creek. Her chest was bloody from a briar-sliced ear, a pink tint that the Bald Eagle hadn't quite washed off. When she started following scent and skidded to a stop and darted to one side, I figured she'd found a laggard woodcock. What flushed was a grouse. It came out on the far side of a briar patch, its wet wings thrashing. The grouse looked black in the dim light. It flew low, and at first I couldn't shoot because Jenny was in the way. Then the bird put some air under its wings. It slanted to the right, turning its back toward me. At my shot, it splashed into the creek.

Jenny jumped in and started paddling. Her head with its white blaze lay low in the muddy water. The current swept her downstream. Gradually she gained on the grouse, a tiny dark lump floating on the slick surface. I walked along in a muddy cornfield bordering the creek. With Jenny, I never doubted she would get a bird once I'd brought it down. In fact, I had become lazy about marking down fallen birds, believing that my spaniel would fetch back whatever I had shot. I watched from a distance as Jenny caught up with the grouse. She took it in her mouth and turned toward the bank. Swimming hard and heading upstream, she could not quite hold her own against the current. She edged sideways, coming closer to the bank. When she climbed out, she did not stop to shake off but came straight to me, walking steadily, her sides heaving, water dripping from her chin and the tips of her ears and running down her chest. Her eyes were riveted on mine. She laid the grouse in my hand.

~

"Caillie." She shoots me a glance and quickly turns her head away. She stares into the brush. I reach down and pat her head. My touch breaks her fixation, and she wags her tail while lowering her ears and pushing her head up into my hand. I tell her to slow down, take it easy, keep close. Sometimes speaking at length to a dog and letting her know that you are paying attention—that you're not angry at her, or putting too much pressure on her—is enough to get her focused. Enough to let her remember that she's half of a team and not a wild predator working on her own.

In this instance, it seems to do the trick. As we probe farther into Everyman's Covert, Caillie stays in close, working generally back and forth, checking out the likely spots: a sprawl of brambles off to the right, a thicket of gray dogwood on the left. She loops out in front, turns back toward me, and quarters into what little breeze is stirring. We proceed through the cover. Which, in this, the first week of the grouse season, is simply too thick to hunt effectively. It feels like summer in here. The temperature hovers in the sixties. We haven't had a frost yet, and the dense grass and weeds must mask any bird scent. So few leaves have fallen from the trees that if a bird does flush, it is likely to be heard and not seen. Grouse season commences in mid-October in Pennsylvania, which is about two weeks too early. Yet rarely can I resist going out.

We hunt east along the old field's uphill edge, avoiding where we can the shoals of thorny multiflora rose that are slowly expanding through Everyman's Covert. We cross a ditch that leads down to the creek—sometimes it's a torrent, but in this dry year it's a rock-studded gully. Where the brush peters out against the open woods, we stop and turn left. We hunt downhill along the edge of the cover until the creek is in sight. Then we turn left again and head back in a westerly direction. Most of the time, Caillie works within a reasonable distance; it's warm enough that she has begun to pace herself, slowing down on her own. She's panting, which makes it tough for her to take in and process scent. Nowhere in the covert does she indicate the presence of game: her tail does not speed up, nor do her movements become more animated and intense; she does not "get birdy," as we say.

The creek is low and sluggish. Caillie wallows where the water pools between gray rocks topped with dried algae and mud. She laps up a long drink. The water slips past us in two channels, giving off a mild and not unpleasant tang of decay. I have seen the Bald Eagle out of its banks and roiling through the fields, its oxbows and backwaters become ponds and lakes; but it hasn't been that way for a long time, as Pennsylvania and much of the Northeast have been locked in a drought for several years.

If we find any birds today, I expect they will be on this lower side. Here the soil is dry and hard in the open places, but it remains damp and inviting in the shade beneath the trees.

As the years have passed, I have found fewer woodcock in Everyman's Covert. That could be, in part, because the woodcock population has been slowly diminishing throughout the range of the species. It could also come from the fact that the trees at Everyman's have grown taller, their crowns knitting together and becoming more dense, and openings in the brush— the singing grounds where woodcock conduct their spring mating ritu- als—have become choked with stems no longer being grazed back by cows. I would bet there hasn't been a cow pastured in this field in half a century. Woodcock season has not yet begun, so if Caillie should happen to flush one of the long-billed birds, I'll not shoot at it. Any woodcock we might happen onto would likely be a local bird, an adult or a bird of the year from a brood raised in what little decent woodcock breeding cover remains. Later in the fall, I'll be back in hopes of finding flight birds: woodcock coming from places farther north, migrating through the valley, headed for wintering grounds hundreds of miles to the south.

Caillie and I draw a blank. Once I thought that I'd heard a grouse rumble in the distance, but the dog never indicated any scent. I'm not surprised. Perhaps the grouse are keeping cool in the shade of the deep woods, or under the hemlocks farther up the slope: I'm too tired and sweaty to go find out. Or perhaps there aren't many birds around, and it will be another lean year for grouse. Perhaps no woodcock hatched in Everyman's Covert in the spring of 2002. Perhaps they never will again.

~

At the truck, after giving Caillie a bowl of water, I open the door to the crate and tell her "Kennel up." She springs up onto the tailgate and goes inside the dog box. I unload and case my shotgun and put it behind the seat in the cab. Turning onto the highway, I drive east, up Bald Eagle Mountain. This long, looming ridge is also known as Muncy Mountain, because it rises at its northern end near the town of Muncy, near the great bend in the West Branch of the Susquehanna River, some seventy miles northeast of Centre County, the place where I was born and where I have lived almost all of my life.

At the top of the mountain, I wait for a break in the traffic, then turn left into the parking lot of a chiropractor's office. When I was a boy, this building housed a restaurant, although I can't recall my family ever eating there. An ice-cream stand stood a bit farther down the road; only a concrete slab remains where it once perched at the mountain's brink. Both the stand and the restaurant looked out over the broad bucolic valley.

This area where the highway crests Bald Eagle Mountain is known locally as Skytop. When I was about twelve years old, my mother gave me and my younger brother permission to ride our bicycles from the town where we lived, State College, all the way to Skytop, about five miles away. We took along water in our Boy Scout canteens. Mom packed us a lunch, which we carried in our bikes' metal panniers. We ate sitting under a tree along the side of the road. An occasional car passed by; the drivers looked at us, and some of them waved. We had to push our bikes up the last mile of the grade. Mom came along in the green Chevrolet station wagon and met us on top. No doubt we talked her into ice-cream cones at the summit stand. With the volume of traffic that uses the road today, a bicycle trip like that one would be almost suicidal. Forty years have passed since Mike and I biked to Skytop, an event that now seems to have happened in a different age and a different world—which, in a way, I suppose it did.

In the parking lot I stand on the hot pavement and look out over the valley. On the far side of the vale about three miles distant, the Allegheny Front extends as a long blue horizon. From Bald Eagle Creek, on the valley floor seven hundred feet below, a series of narrow parallel hollows branch off to the northwest, climbing gradually toward the Front. The hollows are a mix of fields and trees. Separating the hollows are long, mostly wooded hills. The hollows and hills end just below a bench of land running parallel to and a few hundred feet lower than the Front. My house sits on that continuing, forested bench. Beyond the Front lies the Allegheny Plateau, high, rolling, and profoundly wooded. Bald Eagle Valley runs northeast to southwest; as a landform, it represents the westernmost valley in the Valley and Ridge Physiographic Province of Pennsylvania. The province comprises an old upland that has been eroded extensively over the ages: the ridges, capped with harder rock than the valleys, have eroded more slowly and thus remain higher. Under various names, Bald Eagle Valley extends well to the south of Pennsylvania, melding with other southwest-trending valleys that eventually lead all the way to northern Alabama, where the Appalachians—the great and ancient mountain chain of which the Alleghenies are a constituent range—fade out into lowlands.

I turn about-face and look in the opposite direction, to where the top of Bald Eagle Mountain once stood. Until this past summer, chestnut oaks, gray birches, and white pines grew in the thin, stony soil on the ridgetop. What I see now is a long flat stretch of rust-colored rubble: the mountain's substance, blasted apart, dug out and shoved aside by huge machines.

About two hundred yards away, a yellow loader labors past. It is longer than a tractor-trailer. Its wheels stand taller than my pickup truck. Its engine roars, and it kicks up clouds of dust. The loader's voluminous bed is heaped with rocks and dirt. Behind it comes another identical conveyance, similarly laden. Between me and the earthmovers, a line of cars files slowly past, bumper-to-bumper on the old road, even as the loaders and trackhoes and bulldozers and dump trucks labor at building the new road, Interstate 99—the highway that, in my mind, epitomizes the way my home has been changed forever.

I look back toward the valley. My eyes play over the familiar hollows. They stop momentarily on my coverts: The Jay Place, Cemetery, Christmas Tree, Porky's. Far to the east, pale behind the haze, Burnt Baker. Down in the valley, Diehard. To the west, not quite visible on account of the lay of the land, Ballfield and Pufferbelly.

Before the year is out, I'll visit all of them.

Chapter 2

The peak of the fall colors seems to be about two weeks late this year. It's October 25, a cool day, cloudy with a drizzling rain and the kind of subdued, general light that shows off to its best advantage the autumnal brilliance of the eastern woods.

Sassafras trees are salmon, gold, banana-yellow—all of those colors on the same tree, sometimes on the same branch. Red maples sport leaves that are gold on their undersides and orange on their upper surfaces; the leaves nod gently as the water drips off them. Basswoods show a subtle greenish yellow, dogwoods are the rich red of burgundy wine. The oaks have finally begun to take on their slow, long-lasting bronze. On the forest floor lies the scattered bluish gray of fallen grapevine leaves—the only hue in that riot of color that foretells the drabness to come.

I smell the strong minty odor of pennyroyal crushed beneath my boots, spicy wild carrot fronds, and apples lying in sweet rot beneath an old tree with a precarious slant to its trunk. If I were a grouse, I'd be after those windfalls—or at least I'd be hanging around nearby.

Caillie leads the way into the brushy woods. We hunt past clumps of multiflora spangled with bright red rosehips. Past the equally vivid scarlet fruits of barberry. There's food aplenty in this covert. It remains for us to find the birds that ought to have been drawn here by the provender.

A band of robins interrupt their foraging to scold us; their ruddy breasts seem pale compared to the colorful foliage. At my feet, what appears to be a shrew goes dashing along through the leaf litter. The creature is a quick brown blur that vanishes beneath the leaves, only to reappear momentarily at the base of a fallen branch and then to dive out of sight again, like a half-formed thought that the mind cannot quite apprehend.

In front of us, turkeys cluck in the foggy woods, and Caillie runs amok. I can hear their wings flogging as she puts them into the air. She gives out several excited yelps. I don't even bother trying to whistle her in, because I know she would ignore me. I lean against a tree and wait, only mildly annoyed at my strayaway bitch: Jenny would have done the same. After a while, Caillie comes trotting back. She sits down beside me, soaking wet, wagging her tail, her eyes half shut, her lips drawn back in a canine grin. She looks at me out of the corner of her eyes. As a dog, she knows it's much more profitable to seek forgiveness for an action rather than to ask for permission. In the distance I can hear the *kee-kee* calls of young turkeys desirous of getting back together again. If I had a box call, I could probably toll one in.

But I'm not hunting turkeys today. For one thing, the season hasn't opened on them yet. And turkeys are suspicious birds with incredibly sharp eyes and ears: to hunt them effectively requires that you dress in camouflage clothing and move furtively through the woods, stopping and hiding before trying to call them in. Turkey hunting is too static for me. I would rather range about, seeing something new every minute. Plus, in Pennsylvania it is illegal to use a dog for hunting turkeys—perhaps because it confers an unfair advantage on the hunter—and much of the satisfaction I get out of hunting comes from working in tandem with a dog. All of these factors have combined to prevent me from hunting turkeys, even though I admire their intelligence and sensory capabilities, and even though they are superb table fare. (I know that, because I once bagged one that flushed like a grouse.)

Caillie and I hunt in a different direction, away from the enticing flock.

The light rain continues to fall. It blurs the outlines of the mountains. A gust shakes the treetops, sending down a sudden shower. Geese pass over, unseen in the clouds, honking softly. Fox sparrows scuffle among the fallen leaves, looking for insects and seeds. Crows caw in the offing.

We proceed along the bench, past witch hazels laden with nutlets and with pale yellow threadlike flowers. (Witch hazel is our only shrub to both fruit and flower in autumn.) Grapevines dangle their clustered ice-blue fruits, triangular beechnuts lie scattered on the ground—good grouse foods all. We work our way uphill between fallen oaks and more tangles of grapevine and big clumps of greenbrier. Caillie checks out all of those potential grouse hideouts. Nothing. Higher up on the mountain we turn and hunt back along the slope above the bench, through equally attractive cover.

An hour later, and we still haven't flushed a grouse. I call Caillie in. I squat down on my hams and support myself by resting the shotgun's buttstock on the ground. Worrying that it will be another poor year makes me cross, and a bit edgy. For six years in a row, grouse numbers have been depressed in central Pennsylvania. In the 1980s and early 1990s, I could be confident of flushing twenty to thirty birds in a day's hunting. On some occasions Jenny and I put up more than thirty-five. I would get shooting at five grouse, maybe ten, and often I would come home with a bird and sometimes with my limit of two weighing down the game pouch.

Then, in 1996, things fell apart.

It's likely the breeding season started off normally that year. The males would have staked out their territories and begun drumming to summon potential mates. With his tail fanned, the cock grouse stands on a prominent log or stump and beats the air with his wings; the rush of air created by the wingbeats sounds like a drum being thumped. The drumming starts out slowly, then increases in speed until the individual beats merge into a steady whir lasting for several seconds. The bird's wings blur, and it looks as if the grouse ought to be lifted into the air by his efforts, but he remains attached to his perch. The sound of drumming can carry up to a quarter mile. If you are eavesdropping at short range, say fifty feet, the drumbeats get inside your chest. You feel like you're being thumped on the sternum with a spoon.

The female grouse comes sneaking coyly in. The hen watches as the male inflates himself like a miniature turkey gobbler, then struts about, hissing and dragging his wingtips on the ground. After mating, the female will go off on her own and nest, sometimes at the base of a tree, or tucked in against a log, a root, a rock. She lays her buff-colored eggs, nine to a dozen of them. Over the years, I've found and photographed several hens on their nests. Usually, they sit tight enough that I can get within a few feet of them.

In the spring of 1996, I remember, a week of cold rain settled in around the time when the grouse chicks should have been pipping their shells. It was so raw that I kept a fire in the woodstove until the middle of May, when usually the last fire is in April. Insects are an important source of protein for developing grouse chicks, and perhaps the weather was sufficiently cold and damp that the insects did not hatch on time or were inactive during that crucial period. Later in the month it got cold again and rained for another long spell. Maybe the young birds that had survived the first bout of bad weather were now a bit too large for their mothers to cover them—to keep them warm and dry—when brooding them. However it may have happened, the grouse population plummeted. In the summer, I found grown birds consorting with each other—not juveniles, but adult hens keeping company because they had no broods to shepherd about. That odd sociability foretold a bleak hunting season; indeed, I found and flushed few birds that fall—so few that, by mid-November, I stopped hunting them altogether. I was afraid that if I removed too many birds from my coverts, the population wouldn't come back for a long time.

The next year brought another cold, dreary spring. In the fall, I found almost no grouse. I shot some woodcock and a few pheasants, mainly for the enjoyment of my old dog, Jenny, and for the edification of my young dog, Caillie. By then, Jenny was nine years old and had started to slow down. Caillie was a youngster, and it was time to get her started on her life's work. But with the grouse so few, we missed some important lessons. Nor was the grouse population appreciably larger from 1998 through 2001.

This year doesn't promise to be a banner year, either. I haven't seen many grouse while hiking or driving on woods roads. Friends who are grouse hunters report spotting a few birds, but not many. And it's not going to be easy for me to get in as much hunting this fall as I usually do.

I write books for a living—an occupation that, while it doesn't bring in much of an income, gives me a very flexible schedule. But now, for the first time in almost twenty years, I have taken a regular job. I am writing for a magazine published by Pennsylvania State University, which lies on the far side of Skytop about twenty miles from my home. I've been hired by the office where my wife, Nancy, usually works: she's on a leave of absence, writing a book of her own. Fortunately, I can do some of the magazine work out of our home, and, to a certain extent, I can still set my own hours. But it's quite different than in the past, when, once the bird season started, I could drop whatever I was doing, pick up the gun, whistle for the spaniel, and head out.

I stand up, look about, and tell Caillie to heel.

As I said, I'm edgy now, as I scan the cover out in front—edgy, because I really want to find grouse. I want to find grouse because there is no other sort of hunting as thrilling and challenging as the pursuit of those wild and cagey birds. I want to find grouse so that Caillie can work out how to handle them. At age six, she has never enjoyed a season with abundant birds, a season when she can make mistakes, learn from her missteps, and arrive at an understanding of how to effectively find and flush grouse.

I want to find grouse—I want there to be birds in my coverts— because this could be my last autumn in Pennsylvania. During the past summer, Nancy and I bought a farm in New England. We had considered leaving Centre County for several years, because of the new roads that were under construction or were being planned, the ever-increasing traffic, the housing developments and big box stores popping up on every hand. We could think about leaving because a particularly cruel event had struck our lives—I'll share it with you later—cutting our emotional ties to the place we had for so long called home.

For several years we had been looking for land. We came close to buying a ninety-acre parcel in northern Pennsylvania, but the deal fell through when we learned that the sellers had leased the mineral rights to a natural gas company. We thought long and hard about a two-hundred-acre farm on Cape Breton Island in Nova Scotia, from which you could see emerald pastures and forested mountains and, to the north, the distant glint of the Northumberland Strait. But the owner, as it turned out, didn't really want to sell, and Cape Breton seemed a world removed from Pennsylvania and the friends we had made there over the decades.

Then, on a rainy day in June, in northeastern Vermont, Nancy hiked up a hill ("There's a beautiful view in that direction," the realtor had said, pointing from inside her car, "but you can't see it just now."), looked around at the undulating land, the mix of hardwood and softwood trees, the hayfields and the potential horse pastures, and said to me, "If you want to move, this is the place." The landscape was beautiful and inviting, and the area reminded me of Centre County thirty years in the past. But I looked at the ramshackle farmhouse, grimaced, and shook my head. Nancy talked me into coming back the next day. Under a blue sky and a bright sun, the house didn't look so impossible. And that view to the north was grand—sharp mountains and deep glacier-cut gaps. Before heading back to Pennsylvania, we made an offer on the property. A month later, we owned 108 acres, the house, a big garage, and a machine shed that could be expanded into a barn.

At the time, we did not know when we would be moving. We needed to look more closely at the farmhouse—should we remodel it, or was it beyond saving? A concrete porch had tilted, channeling runoff from the roof in under the stone foundation. Beneath a separate wing of the house, the foundation was also unraveling, so that the post-and-beam structure it supported looked like it was ready to tumble downhill.

We could fix up the house enough to use it as a summer place. Then, a few years down the road, we could remodel it more extensively. Or we could tear the house down and build a new dwelling. There was an outside chance that we would relocate soon, perhaps as early as next summer, depending on what we decided to do with the farmhouse, and if we could sell our current house—I had built it myself twenty years earlier. Would

Will, our fourteen-year-old son, want to move? When looking at the property in Vermont, we had visited the school serving the local area. It was a beautiful brick academy in the best New England tradition. But Will had roots in Pennsylvania, just as we did. He had friends he didn't want to leave. And he was starting his freshman year at the local high school in Bald Eagle Valley.

So everything is up in the air. We don't know where we'll be a year from now. But one thing at least is certain: It's bird season in the central Pennsylvania uplands. I have a shotgun in my hands, a spaniel straining to hunt, and I want to find her some grouse.

I release Caillie, and we hunt onward through the misty, brushy woods. Using a combination of soft whistle notes and hand signals, I direct her to a grape-festooned blowdown, from which I fully expect her to root out a bird. I post myself on the edge of the tangle, my legs spread slightly apart, ready to shift my weight to one side or another and to point the gun in whichever direction our quarry decides to fly. But Caillie sniffs her way through the grape tangle, slips out on the far side, and keeps going.

The rain steps up. The trees' branches wave in the breeze, and yellow leaves go sideslipping down. We turn and make another pass, a hundred yards higher up on the mountain. An hour later, as I walk out of the brush without once having raised my gun, it occurs to me that this could be the last time I hunt this covert.

~

Most hunters name the places where they hunt for grouse and woodcock. I'm no exception to that rule, but, as it happens, the covert we have just beaten through so fruitlessly does not have a name. I've never taken anybody there, since the landowner was emphatic about giving me and no one else permission to hunt it, and there has never been a need to refer to the spot in conversation. I first tried it out a couple of years ago, after the grouse population had crashed. It lies along the road a couple of miles from my house. It's easy to get to: just park along the berm of the gravel township road, and wade into the

brush. I guess I could call it Frustration Covert, because, although food and cover are both abundant there, I've never killed a grouse in the place.

I have always preferred covert to cover for designating the spots in which I hunt. "Covert" suggests the hidden, secret nature of such places, while "cover" describes the plants growing there, nurturing and sheltering the birds.

Some of my coverts I found by asking deer hunters where they had flushed grouse. I spotted others by driving around, looking for old fields and clear-cuts, then knocking on farmhouse doors and asking permission. (Good entertainment, in and of itself: I have met some true characters, like the old fellow who came out onto the broken porch of his farmhouse, wearing a frayed bathrobe, on his head an unraveling straw hat. I asked if I could hunt for woodcock on his boggy, overgrown acres. He didn't recognize the word "woodcock," but when I described the long-billed bird, he said, "Bogsuckers? Sure, go ahead and clean 'em out.") More than a few of my coverts I located by studying topographic maps, the kind with the green overlay designating woods. On foot, I explored isolated pockets of white (open ground) set back in the forest away from roads, and often those sunny islands proved to be old pastures and cropfields grown up in brush, creating the fertile, diverse transition zones of vegetation that grouse love. I checked out dotted lines that represented old roads wandering through the woods. Sunlight streaming down to those overgrown tracks provided, on either side, narrow strips of thick vegetation, linear bands of cover in areas where birds were otherwise scarce. Walking the roads—one of the easiest and most pleasurable ways to hunt—yielded frequent open shots.

To the uninitiated, grouse cover may seem like so much featureless brush, but the hunter soon learns to recognize its hard-to-explain but definitely "birdy" look. I remember the first time I tried a section of land scraggy with aspen, pitch pine, and scrub oak. That was before I had Jenny. I stepped slowly through a swale where the aspens still twirled a few gold leaves and fallen grapes lay scattered on the ground. "This place *has* to have grouse," I said aloud, and at that moment a brown blur detached itself from the leaf duff and went clattering off between the trees. It was very much an instinctive shot, to which my brand-new short-barreled 20-gauge was well suited: swing and overtake and punch the trigger, the right barrel transfixing the bird in a cloud of feathers. I was so proud of that grouse—proud of recognizing a productive grouse covert, as well as taking a bird from it—that I carried it home to my parents' house and helped my mother prepare it for the table.

To be a grouse covert, a tract of land must possess two critical features: vegetation that offers food, and vegetation that affords cover. Also, in my experience, a grouse covert should include a component of wildness. Although it may border a farm or be traversed by a road, the land should be sufficiently remote that the grouse are not forever being bothered by humans. If I could assemble an ideal covert, it would include (preferably in several hundred acres) evergreens, both scattered and in dense clumps, among whose boughs the birds could loaf during cold and wind and rain. Blackberries pushing up where logging had removed mature hardwood trees, and piles of tops from the cut trees, where the birds could huddle.

Small grassy clearings where mother grouse could take their broods to find insects. Plenty of berry-producing shrubs and vines. And, selfishly, I would want some open lanes—old logging roads are nice—through which the flushed birds would dart, giving me chances to shoot.

Over the years, I found many such places in Bald Eagle Valley. Today, some of those coverts remain productive; others do not. Some are now ringed with NO TRESPASSING signs. Several of my choicest spots have become cornfields. More often, new houses or trailers sit in the middle of my old hunting grounds.

As I said, almost all of my coverts have names. At Porky's, a partner's aggressive German shorthair met up with the swiping tail of a large porcupine. At Doll Baby I found a broken porcelain doll amid the trash from a collapsed house. One day my friend Carl and I were hunting a new, unnamed covert near the railroad that runs down the valley when an excursion train came chugging past, its cars drawn by an antique steam engine. We dubbed the place Pufferbelly.

Fox Pup got its name following an encounter with a grizzled turkey hunter who asked if we'd heard that fox pup yappin' a few minutes before. The "fox pup" was actually my friend Dale's springer spaniel—Ginger is so wild for grouse that she often barks shrilly when they flush, an action that would disqualify her at a field trial but that can be a distinct advantage in thick cover.

Sometimes the macabre creeps into the naming process. A nosy, officious fellow named Baker lived at the mouth of a hollow where I often hunt. Baker did not own the land, but he felt the need to quiz me every time I went there, and to brag of his poaching exploits. He died in a house fire that apparently started after he fell asleep while smoking a cigarette in bed. Burnt Baker, we call the place today.

Grouse and woodcock coverts are the very foundation of my hunting. They are fragile places, and I don't share them casually. Too many hunters can make grouse flighty and wild. Removing too many grouse can suppress a local population and ruin the hunting for years to come. When I go tramping through my coverts, I like to take home game every now and then, but that's not the only reason I preserve their sanctity. For me they are points of concentration—of birds, experiences, memories—places too precious to be bandied about.

A few years back, a particularly inquisitive neophyte grouse hunter buttonholed me and asked where I hunt. "Bald Eagle Valley," I told him. "Yes," he said, "but *where* do you hunt." "Bald Eagle Valley," I repeated. "I know," he said, "but *exactly* where do you hunt?" I sighed, before pronouncing each word slowly and carefully: *"Bald. Eagle. Valley."*

Chapter 3

We call this covert Diehard. Carl named it. Because, as he put it, only a diehard would slosh through the creek to get to the forty-acre patch, the way we did on that November afternoon almost two decades back. It had rained all day, and we were drenched. At half-past three the lowering sky was growing dim. Calmer, more rational souls would have kept driving down the valley, headed home to peel off sodden clothes and take steaming showers and sit near the woodstove with a restorative cup of coffee. But I had mentioned to Carl that I'd found woodcock in the old pasture, and he would have a go.

Now it is a cool, cloudy Saturday morning in late October. Carl isn't with me on this hunt, although he'll be here for a week later in the season. I heel Caillie along between the railroad tracks, step over the left rail, and go slip-sliding down through the railbed's fist-size limestone chunks to the water's edge. Today the wading will be easier. Much. Although the clouds are thick, it isn't raining; nor has it been raining for three solid days, as it had done that time in the 1980s, and the water is not brown, roiling, and freighted with branches and trash. I don't need a stick for the crossing, as I did that time with Carl—even supporting myself with a stout length of wood, it had been dicey whether I'd make it without taking a header.

However, it was worth it: we each killed a woodcock. I remember the bird I took. Jenny was quartering through the cover, and she had just turned and begun heading back toward me when she made game. The woodcock, after it flushed, flew straight at me. Dun-colored mud adorned its beak almost all the way to its base. The bird swerved past me and went skimming away. As it lifted over a stand of crabapples, I took my shot.

Now, accompanied by a different spaniel, and on a very different sort of day, I cross the Bald Eagle at a broad, shallow stretch. Only in the middle must I splash through a yard or so of quiet water, which doesn't come near to my boot tops. On the far side, while loading the gun, I realize that I've forgotten my whistle. I keep it on a lanyard, hung on a peg in the mud room next to my shooting vest, and I must not have grabbed it on my way out the door.

Caillie is obedient to the whistle, always has been. That fireplug-shaped piece of black buffalo horn is my one deterrent to her power and speed. I wonder how she'll hunt in the absence of that reminder, the small note that can (usually) thwart her desire to race on ahead, and keep her working close to the gun.

I hup her. I clamp her cheek between my thumb and forefinger and lift up her head, so that she has no choice but to stand on her hind legs and look the master in his ominous, penetrating eye. "You will keep close," I tell her. We've worked a lot on that command, Keep close. It means stay in front of the gun, quench your exuberance, ignore the urge to run hard and recklessly, do not heed the field-trial imperative bred into your bones. Mainly, it means *remember the man with the gun.*

I let her go, then make up to her by stroking her ears and telling her she's a good dog. We push ahead into the dry stalks of goldenrod. I keep her at heel for the first twenty yards. Then: "Hup." After a wait of ten or so seconds, I heel her back to where we started off, hup her again, wait until she's looking at me, then give the command she's been waiting for: "Hunt 'em up." As soon as she gets ten yards out, and before she can build up a head of steam, I call out a sharp, guttural "ehhh," meaning *no, cease, desist,* then whistle two notes using my mouth. She turns back in, passing across in front of me. She looks at me: Am I doing okay? she seems to say. "Good girl," I tell her. We move on, and she hunts within a reasonable range, which results in her checking out cover she might otherwise have missed when barreling down the field.

No shiny red fruits adorn the hawthorns, perhaps because of the drought. Beneath the crabapples I find no greenish white, puddled woodcock droppings. It is still in advance of the woodcock season—I'm out here hunting for grouse, but I'm also conducting a reconnaissance to see if there are any locally grown woodcock in Diehard, which was once a superb, if smallish, 'cocking ground. In the open parts of Diehard the goldenrod is thick; even in springtime, after winter's snows have crushed the stems down, I imagine it would be hard for a male woodcock to find a clearing in all of this vegetation—a clearing where he might sit, observable by females, and sound his *peent* call, his stark invitation to mate. And from the edges of Diehard, the forest is closing in, casting its shade on the ground. This covert, like Everyman's just a mile down the valley, is passing by, becoming overmature, no longer offering woodcock the habitat they require to breed and raise their young.

We make a loop and hunt along the perimeter of Diehard. All the way around the covert we go; then we strike out through the middle. Down and back again, in a thorough coverage. Not a woodcock or grouse do we find. The only sign of life is a mixed flock of passerines—a half-dozen sparrows, a male and a female cardinal, and several drab thrushes. My eyes pass over them in a cursory fashion, concentrating as I am on the possible flush of a gamebird.

~

Around noon I find a log near the creek, sit down, and eat a sandwich. The sun breaks through the gray, gilt-edged clouds. It flashes off the water, then dims again as the clouds slip back in front. Along the curving corridor of the Bald Eagle stand big sycamores. Their massive trunks are brown at ground level; above the brown zone are mottled patches of white, lemon, pale green, and tan, the crazy-quilt colors showing through where scraps of the outer bark have flaked off. The trees' upper branches are a smooth pale buff, almost white. They make the trees look like forest specters raising their arms in the air. In the creek, fallen sycamore leaves float by. Some of the leaves sit like small tan boats on the surface of the stream, and others, submerged in the greenish water, twirl slowly past.

This would be a nicer spot if not for the tractor-trailers growling on U.S. Route 220, half-hidden by trees across the creek. In the last ten years, traffic on the road has probably doubled. There are some very good reasons for building better highways in Centre County. My son rides a school bus on that road every day. I think about it a lot, the trucks and buses and cars all mixed together, going sixty on a winding two-lane that sits more or less on top of a wagon road created a century and a half ago for vehicles moving at five miles an hour. Highway planners hope that the new interstate will draw about half of the long-haul trucks off of Route 220. They hope the new road will alleviate "projected traffic increases." On the other hand, the new highway will also create its own users: travelers who want to speed up their journey will begin to follow the route. Companies will relocate to the valley to take advantage of the improved access, allowing trucks to deliver supplies and haul away the things that the companies produce. There will be an influx of people to work for the companies, people who will build houses, add their own vehicles to the crush, create a demand for more stores, more restaurants, more gas stations, more doctors' offices and churches and schools—the list goes on and on.

Right now, five miles south of here, on the other side of Bald Eagle Ridge, an event is taking place that I vaguely considered attending. However, I'm much happier to be sitting on this log, a bit leg weary, looking out at the creek and the sycamores, trying to ignore the trucks' thump and whine by listening instead to the wind combing through the trees' crowns, a wood duck's phantom whistling, and a blue jay's squeaky-hinge call. I'm happier having spent half a morning rummaging through what is apparently another blank covert, and sitting here now with not a lot of hope that I'll find many birds after lunch.

They're billing the event as a "Roll & Stroll on the New Interstate 99." The state highway department is letting people walk and bicycle on a recently completed five-mile section of the highway, which will open to traffic in less than a month. I expect folks will be quoted in the newspaper tomorrow, commenting on how the interstate will make their commutes to work shorter and more convenient, and on how the road will lead to more development and jobs and will be a boon to the local economy. They will express their hopes that the highway will give rise to more stores, providing a greater variety of shopping opportunities. (I don't need to buy Alaskan king crab legs or dried chanterelle mushrooms or sushi in the supermarket. I don't need to choose from a dozen brands of strawberry jam. Really.)

If I joined the strollers and bikers, what I would see in my mind's eye would be the farmland lost forever. The brushy draws where my beagles and I once hunted rabbits, now smoothed out and covered with split-levels and ranch houses. I would consider—mourn, to be exact—the spotted salamanders and hognose snakes and box turtles and wood frogs that used to live where that double ribbon of concrete now lies on the land. I'd see the white-oak woods on the north end of State College—where I once spent a summer evening watching a pair of pileated woodpeckers excavating their nest chamber—obliterated in favor of a shopping center within easy access of the new road. I would notice the convenience stores with their garish red awnings cropping up at the interchanges. I would see the desolation of four broad lanes carving their way through the limestone valley and cutting through the familiar wooded ridge.

I would remember driving home from town one night and looking up at Bald Eagle Ridge; I was startled to see a fire, with orange flames leaping high into the black sky. Drawing nearer, I realized that the flames were coming from an immense pile made from the limbs and trunks of the birches, pines, and oaks that had once covered the mountaintop.

I would remember the day I was headed in the opposite direction, over Skytop toward my temporary job. There was a concrete barrier down the center of the road on my left; on my right were the bare earth and broken rocks of the interstate excavation, along with a few remaining tatters of weeds and brush. On the berm of the road, something small and brown caught my eye. A woodchuck had flattened herself in the gravel, waiting for the danger to pass. Her four young crouched belly down just behind her. With a tractor-trailer on my back bumper, I couldn't stop. In any case, there wasn't a thing I could have done. The woodchuck was trying to lead her young to safety, which she imagined lay on the other side of the road. The concrete barrier down the middle of the road stood four feet high. The woodchuck could not know there was no way for her to get past the barrier. She waited, frozen in place, as the car ahead of me sailed past. I am not particularly enamored of woodchucks—I have shot them without hesitation when they were raiding our garden and digging holes in our horse pasture. But as I drove past the mother and her young, my car one in a line of two or three dozen cars and trucks, a knot formed in my stomach, a knot that would not go away for a long time.

~

Caillie and I head south, leaving Diehard behind. We hunt through an area of poorer cover on the flats just up from the creek. It's mainly open woods, with scattered clusters of hemlocks, white pines, and leggy rhododendrons, plus some spring seeps surrounded with low red-stemmed willows and yellow-leafed barberry shrubs and a few thinning patches of blackberry. We pass clusters of white and purple asters growing at the edges of little openings. A barred owl hoots from farther up the creek, probably from a stand of hemlocks I can just see in the distance. (Barred owls are the most vocal of our owls: they call at night, and often on cloudy days as well.) Out in front of us, a band of turkeys go running off through the woods. Before Caillie spots the turkeys, I make her hup. The birds' bodies are dark and lanky, and their naked heads are bluish. Turkeys thrive in mature woods, whereas grouse prefer younger, brushier habitats. I have seen more turkeys than grouse in my coverts over the last several autumns, which tells me that my hunting spots are getting old and past their prime.

On the other hand, I've also spent many hours tramping through perfectly fine grouse habitat—tracts that were logged eight and ten years back—and still encountered few grouse.

I heel Caillie, not wanting her to get wound up chasing "skinheads," as I sometimes disparage *Meleagris gallopavo*, to the annoyance of my turkey-hunting friends.

We potter along through the thin cover, finding nothing. We turn uphill and loop back through the woods toward Diehard. We give the covert another good, wandering pass, again failing to raise a bird. I'm wasting my time here: I decide to head back to the truck. Before crossing the creek, I unload my gun. I have just slipped the cartridges into a front pocket of my game vest when, out of a streamside patch of mountain laurel about twenty yards away, there walks a grouse.

The grouse stops on the gravelly bank and looks at us. Quietly, I tell Caillie, "Hup." The grouse stretches its neck and raises its head. Every feather seems to stand out on the bird, from its pantalooned, cream-colored legs to its gold-barred breast, its glistening blue black shoulder ruffs, the spiky brown crest on its head. The grouse is so alert, so pumped up, that it looks positively inflated: about twice as big as a grouse ought to appear. With an unloaded gun, I have a marvelous opportunity to study the bird. The dark eye, bright, liquid, and orbicular. The way, when the grouse takes a step forward, its head jerks along, as if in syncopation, an instant behind the rest of the body.

Can I—possibly—load the gun?

Slowly, I reach for my pocket.

With a soft thrumming of wings, the grouse takes off. It flies across the creek, glides through a stand of brushy woods, and banks to the left. It lands in an old orchard, on the edge of a brushy field ringed with SAFETY ZONE signs next to a farmhouse.

Chapter 4

What I have written about Caillie so far may suggest a half-wild nuisance of a canine. I don't feel that way about her. To the extent that she is an imperfect hunter of birds, I am an imperfect trainer of dogs.

Caillie is short for Capercaillie, her registered name. A capercaillie is a large black grouse found in Scotland and northern Europe; it is also the name of a Celtic band whose music I enjoy. Dogs have a way of picking up nicknames, and Caillie is "Sizzle" almost as often as she is Caillie—Sizzle, because she likes to rest with her head in close proximity to the woodstove, so close that once, when she was a puppy, she sizzled off all the whiskers on one side of her snout. Sizzle also sums up her pert and enthusiastic nature. The dog is also known as "Needlenose" and "Snipenose," in recognition of her narrow, pointed muzzle, which she often pokes inquisitively into shrubs and holes in the ground.

Like most springer spaniels, Caillie is colored liver and white, the dark brown liver hue arrayed in patches against a largely white body. It's an effective color scheme for a hunting dog: I can readily spot the white in the brush, and the liver markings stand out against snowy ground. Caillie has a white blaze on her forehead, long ears quilted with dark fur, and alert, expressive eyes. Brown spots freckle her white muzzle and the fronts of her forelegs. She weighs thirty-eight pounds, and, when she's not cringing, her back stands at about the level of my knees. Her loins and hind legs are thickly muscled. She can leap high, turn suddenly, and sprint at an impressive rate of speed.

Lying down, Caillie will often cross her front paws and rest her chin on them daintily. She is quiet and polite around the house, and is generally obedient. Her manner could be described as "fawning." She is extremely, one might even say ludicrously, submissive—she will drop to her belly and avert her eyes in the presence of a ten-week-old puppy. She was the most submissive puppy in her litter, the one the other dogs picked on, and the one that was assigned to me. I may have been the only actual hunter to have bought a dog out of the breeding, which was between a pair of field-trial champions. The other, bolder pups—perhaps more apt to excel in trials (although I think Sizzle would impress a lot of judges)—went, if I remember correctly, to people intending to campaign their dogs rather than hunt with them. I guess I didn't do my homework fully enough before taking a pup from that litter. An acquaintance who is knowledge-able about field-bred spaniels later described the sire and dam as "two of the hottest trial dogs in the country."

Although timid around other canines, Caillie is savage and merciless toward animals smaller than she. When she can slip out of the yard, she delights in catching and killing chipmunks and squirrels; she will dig determinedly to drag a chipmunk from its den. I have taken her on walks in the woods, and, before I could react to stop her, she has dashed in, nabbed a chipmunk on the ground, and killed it with a bite. Once she tried to run down a fawn in our pasture. When I saw what was happening, I shouted at her to hup. Caillie paid me no heed but went on chasing the fawn, trying to figure out where to seize the blatting, dappled prey (the hind leg? the neck?), which was almost as tall as she but much frailer. The fawn kept running in a circle, bleating piteously, with Caillie on its heels. I ran after both, shouting myself hoarse. (The neighbors later told me they almost called the police.) Finally, I realized I could cut across the circle and tackle my dog. Another time Caillie came trotting back from the pasture, her head up and her tail wagging, a wild turkey poult—dead, and quite a burden—clamped in her jaws. A friend who is a novelist once remarked on how demure Caillie is. I replied that she is indeed demure, "except when she's killing something." My friend laughed and said she would just steal that observation for one of her characters, and I presume Capercaillie has appeared in a fantasy novel since, perhaps as a princess with a taste for blood.

Our house sits in a clearing adjoining a three-acre horse pasture that we created in the middle of our thirty acres of woods. The house is at the end of a driveway about a hundred yards long, leading down from the township road. Caillie does not usually venture as far as the road, which means I can turn her out-of-doors to do her business at night. Sometimes I go out with her, to look at the stars, or listen to toads trilling in Oak Pond or great horned owls hooting from the mountain. One fragrant spring night, I accompanied Caillie outside. All was calm—until she took off like a shot. She raced toward a shrubby black gum, leaped upward, and then sat at the base of the tree, her tail wagging as she stared fixedly into the crown. When I went to the tree, I saw a cat about eight feet up, with all four legs wrapped around the trunk. The cat was shaking with fear. It would not look down. I got the distinct impression that Caillie wanted me to shake the cat down, so that she could pounce on it. The acrid smell of cat urine hung in the air—Caillie had scared the piss out of the cat. Unfortunately, the piss had rained down on the spaniel. A session with the garden hose and dishwashing liquid followed. For days thereafter, whenever Caillie was let out, she would run straight to the gum tree and sit beneath it, looking up into the branches.

As I said, Caillie is usually submissive around other dogs. But not invariably so. I went to northern Wisconsin one time to hunt woodcock and grouse. There were five of us, and we and our spaniels all stayed in my friend Dale's cabin. I set my gear—boots, vest, and gun—in one corner of the living room. Caillie lay down next to my kit. One of the other dogs was a handsome black-and-white male named Dewey. When Dewey ventured near my belongings, Caillie would rise silently, grasp with her teeth the loose skin on Dewey's neck, and calmly guide him away; then she would let go of him and return to her self-imposed guard duty. She did this six or seven times. Dewey was the only dog she kept away. As a male, he was inclined to tolerate this odd bitchy behavior, something Caillie may have realized. Wisely, she never tried the stunt with any of the other female dogs.

Caillie is also a singing spaniel. For several years after we got her, she never made a peep, perhaps because she was so timid. I even wondered if she knew how to bark. Then my son, Will, and I sang a song to her, one we'd heard at a performance of Charles Dickens's *A Christmas Carol.* For "Ebenezer" we substituted "Caillie Sizzle." As we sang her names over and over again, Caillie began to make a groaning sound. We continued to sing. Caillie lifted her muzzle and croaked. Then a howl issued from her throat. Now, as soon as we sing the first few bars of the song, Caillie joins in.

This sort of quirky individuality is part of what I enjoy about spaniels. I also like their size and the utilitarian aspect of their bodies. I like the way they are always merry and upbeat. When Caillie is doing something she considers fun—whether routing chipmunks, chasing robins, or accompanying me on a walk in the woods—she wags her tail quickly and a lot; when she's really happy or excited, her whole body gets into the act.

I like having a dog around the house. I like to pet the Sizzle, and sometimes I let her sit in my lap. Of course, Caillie is more than a pet: she is my partner in the field, and in many ways she is the key to my success—and my failure—as a hunter.

∼

A springer spaniel is not meant to indicate game by pointing it, in the manner of an English setter, pointer, or Brittany. Rather, the spaniel "springs" the quarry—first finding it by scent, then charging in upon it and flushing it out of the cover where it is hidden—so that the animal may be shot. (In times past, the quarry might have been run down with sight hounds, killed by a falcon, or trapped in a net.) A more modern item on the springer's list of chores is to fetch the game after it is brought down. A springer should have a "soft mouth"; it should clasp the animal between its jaws, firmly but gently so as not to damage the flesh, even if the bird or rabbit is struggling. Caillie did not show a soft mouth when she snagged that half-grown turkey poult in our pasture.

My old Jenny was a master at finding, flushing, and fetching birds: grouse, woodcock, pheasants, ducks. She had an excellent nose and an unvaryingly soft mouth. She could mark birds down—watch where they fell, and go straight there—better than any other spaniel I have seen. She was a diligent, fiery hunter, and she was also smart.

Over the last sixty or so years, springer spaniels have diverged into two separate lines: show and field. Springers sold as pets come largely from show breeding, also called "bench" breeding, because the dogs are displayed on benches during shows. The two styles share the same colors and general marking patterns but otherwise are very different. The field-bred dog is lean, vigorous, and athletic. The show- and pet-style springer is heavier-boned and more phlegmatic—it is not expected to hunt or even to become excited by game, and to select such a dog for field work is usually folly. (Oddly enough, one almost never sees a field-bred springer depicted in sporting art. Instead, we get the long-eared, bulging-eyed show variety. It may be that few artists know the difference between the types. In any case, it's a lot harder to capture a spaniel flushing game than it is to paint—or to photograph—a dog, such as a setter, on point.)

Of course I chose both Jenny and Caillie from field-trial stock. However, often it is not easy to train and hunt with a dog from such a bloodline, because the dog is bred largely, if not solely, to excel in field trials—in essence, a kind of a "show" themselves—and not necessarily to accomplish the *real* hunting that takes place where *real* birds are found, in steep, wallowing, thick, thorny, unkempt cover.

The springer spaniel, and also the slightly smaller cocker spaniel, originated in England. There, both kinds of dogs are popular with people who hunt (or "shoot," as they call the activity, reserving "hunt" to mean riding on horseback after foxes). Keith Erlandson was one of Britain's greatest spaniel trainers and field-trial handlers; I had the pleasure of meeting him at his home on a mountain in northern Wales when I was on a gun-buying trip to Britain about ten years ago. Erlandson was a kind curmudgeon who was not afraid to speak his mind. He once stated: "A pure trial dog that is no shooting dog is, to me, no dog at all."

In the United States, field trials for springers are mainly held on level or gently rolling ground, in fields of knee-high, rather sparse grass, so that the dogs can more easily be viewed by judges and an audience. Spaniels display their drive and speed by questing after pen-reared birds, usually pheasants, that were "planted" in the grass a short while earlier. It can be a real and an ongoing struggle to take a dog of field-trial breeding and curb its propensity to run hard, because the desire to go all-out is part of what catches a trial judge's eye. But in the real world, the world of ruffed grouse and woodcock, a hard-running, wide-ranging spaniel may simply cause birds to flush wild.

I trained Caillie, and Jenny before her, at a shooting preserve about twenty miles from our home. I worked both dogs under the tutelage of the man who owned the preserve, a former field-trial participant, who advocated what I now realize to be field-trial training methods. I would drive to the preserve on most Saturdays in summer and early fall. Often the training consisted of a "three-point drill," in which the handler and dog are in the middle, between a pair of gunners walking along one on each side. Pigeons are used as surrogates for game. The gunners show the birds to the dog, waving them and sometimes throwing them down for the dog to retrieve or flush. Such a method encourages a dog to quarter back and forth between the flanking guns and reinforces a side-to-side pattern (spaniel fanciers call it "east-west") in the dog's hunting. (I discovered, to my dismay, that Caillie naturally has a lot more "north-south" in her than "east-west.") Alternately, we would dizzy the pigeons and hide them in the center of the field, so that the dog would flush them in front of the handler, suggesting that birds are found close to the hunter. Spaniels are much too smart to be taken in by this ploy.

My purposes would have been better served by training my dogs on real gamebirds, and on birds such as pen-raised quail released into thick cover. One can also carry pigeons along during training walks and, when the dog isn't watching, roll one in close at hand for the dog to find and flush. Those measures encourage a dog to put its nose down and sniff for a bird's foot scent, rather than to course back and forth with its head in the air, seeking body scent.

I got Jenny at a time when gamebirds, particularly grouse, were plentiful. I had fewer responsibilities then, and possessed the desire and ambition to work long and hard at training her. After beginning her training on the preserve, I took Jenny back there during the fall and winter gunning seasons and handled her in the field for paying customers. Over the years, Jenny flushed and fetched hundreds of birds—both released pheasants and our native wild game.

I did not train Caillie as diligently as I did Jenny. In fact, I did not bring either dog to as high a standard as is possible; for example, I did not teach them to be steady. A steady spaniel, once it flushes a bird or sees another dog flush a bird or hears a gunshot or watches a bird fall out of the sky, sits down, or hups, of its own accord. Steadiness is not easy to instill. The moment that the handler must concentrate on shooting a flushed bird— seeing it with clarity, then bringing a shotgun to bear on it—is the very moment when the dog, suddenly without direct supervision, must remain exactly where it was when that enticing bird took to the air. Not all spaniels that have been steadied are steady all of the time. Springers competing in field trials are expected to be steady, and if they are not, if they break and chase after flushing a bird, they are removed from the competition.

I had planned on steadying Caillie, and I worked at it for a while. But when I disciplined her for failing to hup at the flush—scolded her, then dragged her back to the spot where she should have sat down after flushing a pigeon and instead had gone kiting off down the field after it—she began to show signs of shutting down. Upon catching a whiff of bird scent, she started to hesitate before running in to flush. She looked as if she wanted to avoid the whole business of hunting, so that she could also avoid being disciplined.

In truth, I did not have the concentration to train a dog at that time: two family tragedies, the unexpected deaths of my mother and a niece, had sapped me of enthusiasm and drive. And so, following the course of least resistance, I backed off from trying to steady Caillie. Instead, I just took her hunting, which should have been balm for my soul in those dark days, but often was not. We found few birds in Caillie's formative years, during a low in the grouse population that still hasn't reversed itself. As the years passed, and as one other outdoor activity in particular (riding horses with my wife) began to take up more and more of my time—and, autumn after autumn, as the bird population stubbornly failed to rebound—I never got around to steadying my spaniel. I rather regret not adding that last bit of polish that makes for an exceptional and stylish gun dog.

I plan to steady my next spaniel. I'll try to find a springer that is not out of hot field-trial breeding. Or I might even switch breeds: most field-bred English cocker spaniels instinctively hunt a bit nearer to the gun than the typical springer. I will certainly follow a program of training that ought to contribute to a naturally closer-working dog.

As I recall, it took Jenny about five years to slow down and learn to really use her nose and her brain, to puzzle out how grouse and woodcock behave, and to realize that if she flushed a bird beyond gun range there would be no further reward: no bird to fetch.

Caillie, at age seven, never having hunted during bird-rich autumns, has yet to figure that out.

Chapter 5

One big step lands me on a teetering slab, and the next step places me on the stream's far bank. We've enjoyed several days of much-needed rain, and this freshet, fed by springs in a wooded bowl that lies higher up on the Allegheny Front, runs full and chuckling. It's early in the day. The sun has just risen, and I have a few hours to hunt before I must return home and apply myself to a writing deadline.

With Caillie at heel, I move uphill into the seedling pines and scrubby maples that are slowly reclaiming the fields at Burnt Baker. It used to be that most of my coverts were on old farms like this one; but over the years, many of those places have matured to become woods. Grouse can live in woods, as long as they support a profusion of low, shade-tolerant plants and have some sunny clearings. But a huge deer herd inhabits central Pennsylvania, and in many areas the deer have browsed off all or most of the low plants and tree seedlings, creating an under-story barren of the food and cover that grouse need to survive. These days, most of my best grouse spots are on cutover tracts, where clear-cut logging has bared the land to the sun and where a sudden profusion of stump sprouts, shrubs, and low green plants has gotten ahead of the browsers, at least temporarily. Burnt Baker, probably the best of my coverts, contains a mix of both habitats—reverting fields and logged land.

Moving up the hollow, following my spaniel, I take not the direct path of the hiker but the meandering, halting path of the seeker: the seeker of game, the seeker of nature and self-in-nature. I cast Caillie uphill to check out a grape tangle, a patch of greenbrier, a thicket of gray dogwood. Using the whistle, I draw her back down the slope to work through dense goldenrod, and beneath and between the drooping branches of pines. High above us, a raven mutters. A hidden gray squirrel sounds its hollow knocking, which is picked up by another squirrel, then another, until the whole draw resounds with their calling. Blue jays squawk and scold, then go flashing off through the trees as Caillie hunts past. The sound of traffic on the valley floor is the merest hum.

I wonder if this will be the year when Caillie puts it all together. At the same time, I worry that the apparent dearth of birds will make it unlikely that she'll get enough contacts, enough real work, to show any significant progress. And I wonder how I'll feel about continuing to hunt if it turns out that the grouse aren't around.

The sun climbs above the far slope and shines onto the south-facing hillside where Caillie and I hunt. We could meet with a grouse, and we might also flush a woodcock. I usually run into several of them in Burnt Baker each year, and woodcock season is now open.

The air is chill and clear, with a fresh, clean smell to it. We pass red maples dressed in their finest crimson foliage. As the sun rises higher, the frost-slain leaves on the maples begin to let go and drift down. Everywhere the ground is covered with colorful leaves, and more of them are flurrying with each breath of the wind. I proceed from flaming maple to leaf-twinkling aspen to winter-bare ash in a matter of ten steps. I hup Caillie so that I can stop and study the end-notched leaves of a tuliptree. The English settlers of this land likened the leaf's shape to an old woman's smock. Now, the tuliptree's leaves are a rich, uniform yellow. I put a couple of the leaves in my game pouch to take home for Nancy.

We hunt uphill until we reach the burned-out stone foundation where Baker—numbed by alcohol, I hope—drew his last searing breaths. We skirt the shards of broken glass, the uncapped stone-lined well, the smashed ladder, the remarkably undamaged television satellite dish. I wonder what became of Baker's wife; a thin, silent woman with a child on her hip, she would sometimes step out onto the porch of the ramshackle house when her husband had me tied up in conversation. It seemed to me that a man and a dog represented a diversion to her, a break in the boredom of living in a rundown house in a brushy hollow with a blatherskite husband. Once Baker asked if he might look at my gun, and I winced when he shut the action with a loud snap. He told me of the turkeys he'd ambushed up on the hill. He bragged about confronting trespassers and booting them off the land. According to the newspaper account of the fire, Baker's wife was not in the house at the time of the blaze. I wonder if she'd left him by then and moved into town.

A bank of low pearly clouds comes sliding in from the west, shutting out the sun. The wind picks up, and the air grows chill.

We found no grouse—nor any woodcock—in the excellent cover on the quarter-mile sidehill leading from the parking spot to the jumbled, scorched foundation.

I have pressing work at home, and I really should stop here and walk back down the lane to the truck, but the big bowl higher up on the slope beckons. Caillie and I angle up toward it through a brushy crease in the hillside. We swing around to the west, following the edge of a field dotted with thornapples. We work through a fringe of gray dogwood and ankle-snaring dewberry. I remember the time when a man with whom I had corresponded regarding English shotguns came for a visit, and I took him hunting here. He had the pleasure of meeting and conversing with Mr. Baker. My correspondent friend was from Ohio, where it was flat. He had a trick knee, he told me, and couldn't tackle those steep slopes. So I stationed him where a pair of logging roads met, and suggested that he stand or hunt on the gentler ground thereabouts while Jenny and I climbed and shook the bushes up above. We flushed a cock grouse, which sailed downhill, and I called out, "Bird!" and heard the fellow's shot; but he had missed, and the grouse sailed down the hollow into the pines below.

Caillie and I make one broad, deliberate pass through the logged-off bowl. We hunt into the wind, moving from one grape tangle to the next. At each spot of cover, I hup her, either with a hand signal—she needs to be looking at me to receive that silent, hand-in-the-air command—or, more often, with a whistle pip. I get myself set up in a good area from which to shoot, and release her with a quiet double-pip. Only once does Caillie get really excited. Although she goes over the ground several times, sniffing avidly and wagging her tail, worming through the coiled grapevines, she fails to produce a grouse. Obviously, a bird was there moments earlier: either it flushed wild, or it scampered off before we arrived. When grouse become scarce, they grow wilder. No doubt this response helps to preserve what remains of the breeding population.

We hunt through the best of the cover. This place has been good to me in the past—I've had hunts here when we put up between twenty and thirty birds. But nothing happens today, nothing at all. Caillie and I finish out the cover, turn downhill, and head back toward the fields.

Grouse hunting is work. The harder and the longer you hunt, the more apt you are to roust out birds. And while Caillie and I explored some excellent cover this morning, we haven't hunted it as thoroughly as we might, having left big areas untouched. I know from experience that I can go for long stretches, flush no birds, and then find myself in the middle of sudden, intense action. But I must admit I'm puzzled. We've been out four times this season and have flushed exactly one grouse. We should have encountered dozens. Will it be another terrible year, or have I simply been hunting in the wrong places? Although it hasn't produced many birds in the last several years, Burnt Baker comes as close to being a sure thing as any of my coverts. To have moved only one bird—and that one a distinct "maybe"—is disheartening.

Are the grouse higher up, maybe even on the plateau, feeding on shards of acorns broken up by foraging deer? Are they loafing in the mountain laurel that grows thickly there? Will the birds shift back to the brushy fields and the cutover woods, once the leaves are off the trees and the mountain has gone winter-bare? Or are they closer to hand, tucked away among the boughs of pines and hemlocks, having emerged at dawn to fill their crops with grapes and greens, nuts and buds, and then gone back to bed where they now hold tight and disdain to flush as the dog and I pass below? I don't have a clue.

Burnt Baker is a big four-hour covert, and I only scratched the surface of it, but I scratched a pretty nice part.

~

Driving home, considering the virtue in hunting long and hard, I remember a past hunt. It happened almost a decade back, and the memory centers on a brief moment at the end of a grueling afternoon.

We had slogged through knee-deep snow for hours without seeing a bird. My friend Dale had his year-old pup, Ginger, and I was hunting behind Jenny, Ginger's mother. When we got to the grape tangle, it was Ginger who happened to be in front of me, bounding—almost swimming—through the white powder. She stopped, her nose sunk in the snow, her tail whipping, and I heard the faint stuttering of wings. A grouse flashed up from the snow, then dropped down into it again. Ginger yelped frantically and churned after it. She lunged toward some twisted, half-buried grapevines, and again the grouse hopped up into the air, only to pitch back down again a few yards farther on.

"Wounded bird?" Dale called from behind me.

"I don't know."

Our voices told the grouse that it had more to contend with than a four-legged canine bogged in the snow. Up it came on loud, blurring wings. I would have let Dale take the shot, but I did not know precisely where he was. It did not seem to be a day when we could expect many more opportunities, so, although it was Ginger's first grouse, it was I and not her master who swung the shotgun and dropped the bird.

At the gun's report came the quick beating of a second pair of wings. This grouse, for reasons I still do not understand, flew straight at us, banking past Dale, whose shot sent the bird careering into a snowbank. Then the spaniels were bucking through the drifts to find the birds. Jenny brought me the grouse Dale had shot, and Ginger fetched my grouse for Dale.

It was the perfect end to the day. That one action-filled moment was the reward for keeping the faith and continuing to hunt, for working when you are not sure your efforts will pay off.

I remember how, on that chill afternoon, I took the bird from Jenny, dusted the snow off it, and put it into my game pouch. Then I relaxed and soaked in the surroundings. A sky of a deep, pristine blue. Cold air filling my lungs. Trees creaking on the ridge. A twig of dried oak leaves, lying on the snow, throbbing in the wind like the wings of a dying grouse.

Chapter 6

The bank of clouds that yesterday crept across the sky had thickened by dawn and become a dark gray mass. In the morning, a steady rain began to fall. Around noon, the rain changed over to snow. In the woods outside my office window, the snow worked at knocking the leaves off the maples and black gums.

I'm working at home today, and by the middle of the afternoon I'm done with my assignment. When I turn off my computer and head for the mud room, Caillie shadows me, whining softly.

With the woodcock season now open, I decide to visit Pufferbelly, a covert that over the years probably has yielded more of these wraithlike birds for me than any other. I drive west on Mountain Road, then turn down Reese Hollow, bypassing the traffic light in Port Matilda. It's striking, how many new houses have sprung up in this and most of the other hollows branching off northward from Bald Eagle Valley since we built our own house twenty years ago. It's happening all over the county, all over the state, all over the country. All over the world. The human population is expanding, claiming more and more of the landscape, using more and more of the finite resources that the earth provides. My own family is part of that expansion. We sectioned off our little chunk of the natural world and built our house on it. We have an effect on the environment by living twenty miles outside of the town and driving to a job there: round trip, forty miles a day, two hundred miles a week, ten thousand miles a year. We own two vehicles, one of them a gas-guzzling pickup truck. I think it is important to examine my personal impact on the planet every now and then, and to make decisions, large and small, that will help keep the world a healthy, natural place (and help keep me properly humble in the bargain). However, I won't let the self-scrutiny and mental sermonizing prevent me from enjoying the tag end of this day in a woodcock covert.

When I reach Route 220, I head west again and, after a mile or so, turn onto a rutted farm lane. The lane leads past a brick-sided barn, one end of which has fallen apart, revealing stacks of moldy hay bales. I ease the truck through a mudhole, clank across the railroad tracks, and park next to the raised barrow of fill on which the tracks are laid. Here in the valley, several hundred feet lower than our home on the mountain, it looks as if it has mostly rained today, although it's snowing now, and the heavy wet flakes are beginning to stick.

In Pufferbelly, snow collects on the pine boughs and the tops of the blackberry canes. It starts coming down harder, the snow mixed with rain. Soon my hunting vest is soaked, and water runs off my waxed-cotton coat and trousers. Scents of wet leaves and sodden earth fill the air. It's cold, and at half-past three the light is already beginning to fade. But I'm glad for this stolen hour's hunt, and Caillie is avid. Together we work through the old sloping fields that are grown up in milkweed and goldenrod and Queen Anne's lace, beneath crabapples and aspens and pines that cluster thickly in some areas and dot the fields in others. Pufferbelly offers a series of old fields interrupted by small patches of woods, some of which have been logged within the last few years. It's a rough-and-tumble, down-at-the-heels sort of a covert, full of memories. And at times—today, perhaps?—full of birds.

Caillie hunts off to the right, toward a powerline right-of-way. I let her check out the edge up there, knowing that if she flushes a bird it will probably fly farther up the mountain. She doesn't find anything, and after a minute I whistle her back across. Her soaked fur sticks up in spikes, her wet head looks even smaller than it usually does, and the water flies off her tail as she wags it. Her tail speeds up, and she crouches for an instant before diving in under a crabapple, and I hear the unmistakable twittering of a woodcock's wings. The bird goes out on the far side of the shrubby tree, too low for a safe shot. The woodcock flies away between the crabapples and the gray-trunked aspens, its wings blurring, its diminutive tail spread, its chunky body tilting to one side and then the other as it dodges the tree trunks, its legs tucked up partway and dangling beneath the belly, the out-sized black-barred head attached to the long tapered bill pointing ahead and slightly downward.

I call Caillie back as the bird flies on into the cover.

"Here, girl." I give her a few pats with my sopping glove. She's shivering, from cold or excitement or both. I've had some excellent hunts at Pufferbelly, for both woodcock and grouse. Straightening, I recall a bird taken here with Jenny. She'd driven the woodcock out of the weeds on the other side of the railroad tracks. I killed it going away, making a longish shot, and the bird fell on the far side of Bald Eagle Creek. Jenny searched at first on the near bank; I could make out her white coat through the brush. I blew on the whistle while raising my hand, and she hupped. I called "Back!" and gave her a hand signal that I hoped she could see. I heard her splash into the water. Silence for a time, and again the sound of splashing of water, and Jenny emerged from the low red-toned willows carrying that little bit of a bird, its head lolling to the side and one brown wing standing up in front of the dog's eyes. And just as my heart brimmed over then, so it does now as I think of the same steadfast trust she showed when, at the end of her life, she lay on a blanket in the mud room, and I cupped my hand beneath her head, her ear thick and warm against my palm, her tail thumping weakly, and the veterinarian pressed the needle into the vein in her leg, and she was gone.

I buried her beneath the trees between the house and the pasture, wrapped in the blanket, the fanned tail of a grouse laid on top.

I remember back farther, to the day I brought Caillie home as a seven-week-old pup. Jenny ran at her growling fiercely, and Caillie scrambled to get away, racing for what looked like a dark and sheltering place—only to tumble into a cellar-window well. After that rude introduction, the two became fast friends. Jenny tolerated all kinds of puppy antics; she played gently, not even growling when Caillie chewed on her ears and jowls. She let Caillie sleep with her in her own box (it got rather cramped in there), even though Caillie had a box of her own in the other corner. I sometimes wonder if part of the problem I had in training Caillie, the difficulty I had in forging a close bond between us and claiming her attention completely, stemmed from the fact that she had fixed her affection so thoroughly on the older dog. As I had, too, come to think of it.

These notions pass through my mind as I stare ahead into Pufferbelly. I hie Caillie on, and it's a struggle to keep her hunting close after that first flush on the woodcock. No other scent in the kingdom of scents excited Jenny quite so much as the smell of a woodcock; not a duck, not a pheasant, not even a grouse. Some dogs will refuse to fetch a woodcock, presumably because of the bird's strong smell, but Jenny never hesitated. Caillie is a good fetcher of woodcock herself.

She gets too far out, and I whistle her back in.

The cover changes from an old field to a scourged, cutover woods strewn with broken limbs, shattered trunks, and humped-up roots—logging debris further complicated by a growth of multiflora rose and blackberry. I'm thinking we should have reflushed the woodcock by now, and suddenly the bird is up, this time starting on its own. I'm a whisker too slow in raising the gun and pushing the safety forward, and I fail to trigger the shot before the bird dodges behind a pine.

We keep moving, keep hunting, as the light slowly goes out of the sky. Caillie flushes another woodcock—perhaps the same one, although I don't believe so—and this time I can't get the safety off because my gloved thumb, soaking wet, slips across the top of the knurled knob without clicking it forward. The bird was in the open, offering a very makeable right-to-left shot. The glove goes into my vest. I blow on my cold fingers and try to dry off my hand by sticking it into my pants pocket. Twenty yards farther on, Caillie swerves toward a pine. Just as it dawns on me that on such a wet and miserable afternoon a pine is the perfect canopy beneath which a bird should sit, a hen woodcock flushes. She's big and plump, a clean, pale buff against the drenched brush. I get the gun up and the safety off. The instant that I shoot, the bird jukes left. A clean miss. The woodcock peels back the way we've come, flying west above the railroad tracks, pelting along until she vanishes from sight.

Out on the highway, the cars and trucks have turned on their head-lights. I take the empty shell and the unfired one out of my gun. I bring Caillie to heel, and we walk out onto the tracks and follow the ties back to the truck.

~

I don't mind it much when a woodcock flies off unscathed. With pheasants, I rather resent it when a bird, crowing lustily, outfoxes me. With grouse, I'm apt to be disappointed when I miss, or frustrated, or a little of both. With woodcock—whose manner is reticent and unassuming, and whose numbers have been dwindling for several decades—I am frequently glad to see the bird get away.

The American woodcock is known colloquially as "timberdoodle" (a doodle is a fool, and at times the woodcock can seem naive or foolish); "big eye" (the large eyes serve to gather light at dusk and in the dark, when the bird is active); "bogsucker" and "night peck" (for its habit of probing in soft ground to feed on worms, its favorite food); "hokumpoke" (this one I can't puzzle out); and, somewhat irreverently, connoting its seepy dwelling places and its erratic manner of flying, "mud bat."

Woodcock often hold tight: they don't flush until you're right on top of them. As nocturnal birds, woodcock probably spend much of the day sleeping, and perhaps we hunters wake them up. Often a woodcock will flush, flutter onward for a few yards, set down, and wait as hunter and dog approach again. Thus the shooting can be relatively predictable, and in some cases downright easy—unless you hunt woodcock in thick and thorny places, such as those in which I usually end up pursuing them.

Despite the strong cover that the bird favors, it is generally easier to superimpose a shot pattern on a woodcock than on a grouse, which is overall a faster, warier bird. Judging from the times gunning partners have urged me to take home their woodcock along with my own, the bird is not adequately appreciated as table fare. Perhaps the major attraction of hunting for woodcock lies in the opportunity for good dog work. Pointing dogs lock up solidly on the odoriferous woodcock, which tends not to run away as a pheasant or a grouse often will do. I'm a dyed-in-the-wool spaniel enthusiast, and I doubt I'll ever own a pointing dog, but I will admit that gunning for woodcock over a good setter or pointer is a much easier proposition than taking the birds in front of a flushing dog.

Hunting is only a part of the relationship I have cultivated with this odd, reclusive bird. I know the woodcock as a harbinger of spring, more cheering to me than the most mellifluous thrush. One of my favorite March rites is to watch the woodcock males singing, which they do in an effort to attract a mate. They sing both at dawn and at dusk. The male flies high into the sky; then he starts down in a wide spiral, broadcasting a clear, high sequence of notes that may be represented as *pee chuck tuck cuck oo chuck, pee chuck tuck cuck oo chuck,* on and on as he descends. The song bears some resemblance to the clucking of a robin, except that it is more liquid, resonant, and ethereal. I have always found it hard to imagine the woodcock's flight song issuing from between the bird's knitting-needle mandibles. The singer lands in an opening in the brush and sounds a rasping, nasal *peent,* a come-hither call that sounds much more appropriate to such an oddly shaped, reclusive bird.

Many singing grounds used to be scattered throughout Bald Eagle Valley, mainly on the boggy, marginal farms. Years ago, Steve Liscinsky, a biologist for the Pennsylvania Game Commission, bought some land not far from Pufferbelly; on it he built a shack, to be closer to the woodcock he was studying. Every so often I would run into him in a covert. Liscinsky owned a string of excellent English setters, which he used for finding and banding broods of woodcock in the spring and for hunting woodcock in the fall. A booklet that he wrote, *The American Woodcock in Pennsylvania,* is full of knowledge.

Liscinsky suggested that "the life of a woodcock covert in Pennsylvania is relatively short, at best, about 20 or 25 years. And unlike some woodcock habitats in northern states and Canada, our coverts seldom regenerate themselves on the same site. Instead they change into a forest type through the natural process of plant succession"—a forest whose trees ultimately will shade out the brush that woodcock prefer. Certainly that process is occurring in many of my coverts here in the valley. Others have vanished beneath the plow. A nice little spot that I named Bogsucker Flats is currently a pasture, its new owner having discovered that it wouldn't grow corn very well. I don't know that the interstate is wiping out many coverts directly, but I worry that its location, on the side of Bald Eagle Mountain about two-thirds of the way up, will cut off the water that trickles down the slope—both above and below ground level—to recharge the spring seeps and boggy areas that benefit woodcock and many other wild creatures. And I'm certain that the development that must accompany the new road will destroy many additional acres.

When woodcock habitats are lost, the birds don't simply shift into other settings, because they can live and reproduce nowhere other than in their specialized haunts. The population of the American woodcock, *Scolopax minor,* is falling throughout its range: basically the eastern half of North America from New Brunswick to Louisiana. Probably the decline is caused by ongoing habitat loss, from old farms becoming forests again, and from people usurping the land. There are regulations against destroying wetlands (even seasonal wetlands, and woodcock cover is often classified as such), but developers are good at circumventing the rules. The current administration in Washington has been working for several years to persuade people that seasonal wetlands are not really wetlands at all, trying to declassify them so that builders can drain them and fill them in and put up their developments. Nor do state environmental agencies always work to preserve woodcock habitats. My friend Carl, who lives in southeastern Pennsylvania, is hunting his Rendezvous Covert while it is under a sentence of death by drowning beneath the waters of a dam intended to create a lake at a new state park.

And anyway, who but a hunter (and it seems that fewer of us tramp through the coverts each year) would suggest that an obscure, secretive, worm-eating bird is better to have around than a highway that lets you zip from one place to the next, or a Wal-Mart where you can buy everything your heart desires? Well, maybe not everything. My heart desires peace and quiet and an unmarred natural landscape. It desires more woodcock and more grouse.

~

On the evening after Caillie and I found our first woodcock of 2002 at Pufferbelly, I sat in my livingroom next to the woodstove and remembered one of the odder encounters I have had with *Scolopax minor*.

Several years ago, my friend Tom and I were hunting a new covert that he had just shown me in a side hollow a mile or so north of Bald Eagle Creek. Jenny swept past a patch of gray dogwood whose ruddy twigs held up clusters of ivory white berries. Just then I saw the woodcock. Actually, it had seen me first. On short, wide-set legs it bustled from the edge of the thicket into the center. The bird crouched, facing away from me and yet regarding me, no doubt suspiciously, through eyes that occupied the upper rear portion of its skull. The bird was large, identifying it as a hen. (Female woodcock average 20 to 25 percent larger than males.) Had I not seen the bird running, I doubt I would have noticed it, so perfectly did the wood-cock's plumage blend with the sticks and leaves covering the ground beneath the brush.

I whistled Jenny in, hupped her, and gave her a line: I held my hand forward and, with the fingers extended, arrowed it in the direction I wanted her to go. She charged into the dogwood stems—and ran right over the woodcock. The spaniel kept going, the bird righted itself, shuffled its feathers, resettled, and otherwise did not budge.

Baffled, I hupped Jenny, then brought her back with a series of whistle pips. Straight through the thicket she came, across earth where I'd just seen the wood-cock scuttling. No sign whatsoever that she detected that compelling scent.

Was the bird injured? I'd read that a wounded bird can, as a means of self-protection, instinctively shut off the production of its body scent. By now, Tom had worked his way closer to us. I told him about the woodcock in the dogwood clump. I hupped Jenny, walked around to the far side of the thicket, and waded into it. The woodcock stared up at me through large, dark eyes. Bright droplets of moisture stood out on the horizontal black bars marking the bird's head. Shifting the shotgun to my left hand, I bent over and reached with my right hand. When my glove was less than a foot away from the hen, she lifted from the ground on whirring wings. Not wounded at all! I stood, wrenched up the shotgun, and tried to cover the fast-retreating form. I pulled the trigger, felt the buttstock pound me on the arm, noted that Tom had failed to shoot (it turned out he was screened by some brush), tried in vain to shoulder the shotgun properly, pulled the trigger again—and watched as the woodcock, in full flight, corkscrewed out of sight behind an overgrown fencerow. That was the last we saw of her.

The episode so flustered me that I reloaded the shotgun, with no little difficulty, using an already fired cartridge dug out of my vest. I discovered that little error on the next woodcock flush. Tom, astounded that I wasn't shooting, hastily missed twice, and that bird survived as well.

At least Jenny had scented and flushed it.

Chapter 7

In the preceding pages, I referred to the deaths of my mother and a niece. I do not want to go into those events in detail; I have already written about them in an effort to absorb and understand what happened, and, as much as possible, to put them behind me. But those tragedies had a profound and lasting impact on many aspects of my life, including my desire and ability to hunt.

On September 3, 1995, my mother was murdered. She was stabbed to death by a burglar in her home. The day after she was killed, I found her body. A man was arrested for the crime, and when he came to trial I was subpoenaed to testify. A jury convicted the man and sentenced him to life in prison.

The summer after my mother died, Nancy, Will, and I went to live in an abandoned farmhouse on the coast of Iceland. The trip had been planned for over a year; a book came out of the sojourn, *Summer at Little Lava: A Season at the Edge of the World*. While we were in Iceland, in that pristine, light-filled place, our fifteen-year-old niece died in the crash of TWA Flight 800. Claire was headed from New York to Paris with her high-school French club. Her death, following the loss of my mother, hit hard.

~

In the autumn of 1995, I hunted only a handful of days. It was not that the idea of taking an animal's life repelled me; rather, I lacked the energy and focus to do much of anything. I shot a few birds over Jenny, including several that would have given me greater satisfaction had I not been so weighed down by grief.

One day at a public hunting area in the valley, to the north and east of our home, I shot at a woodcock that Jenny had flushed. I thought I had hit the bird, but I wasn't sure. We went to where the woodcock had slanted down and looked for it for a long time, but we did not come up with the bird: neither Jenny, nor her daughter Tori, nor I, nor Greg, Tori's master and a fellow member of the spaniel hunting club to which I belonged. I'm sure I looked a little askance at Jenny for failing to get that woodcock, because she was usually such a sure retriever. Giving up the search, I picked my hat out of the bush where I'd hung it to mark the spot where the wood-cock had landed. I assumed that I had missed, and that the bird had run on ahead for a few yards and, perhaps hidden behind brush, had flushed again.

We finished out that stretch of cover, then turned to work back in the general direction from which we'd come. I was still bothered by losing the woodcock. I replayed the shot in my mind: the bird had slowed, changed its flight direction slightly, and continued on, flying weakly and gliding down before it had gone very far. I felt sure I had hit the woodcock. "Let's go through that patch of cover again," I said to Greg. We kicked through it, moving slowly. Then Tori took scent: she followed her nose, stuck her head in under some flattened grass, and came out with the woodcock. She gave it to Greg; with a broad smile on his face, he laid the bird in my hand. The woodcock was dead. I turned it over, and there, ringing one grayish, spindly leg, was an aluminum band. I had never shot a banded woodcock before. When I reported the band number to the U.S. Fish and Wildlife Service, they informed me that the bird, a male, had been banded as a juvenile that spring about ten miles north of where I had shot it.

I was using a new shotgun that year, a lightweight 20-gauge side-by-side, an older gun brought over from England. The gun had arrived in the mail a few days after my mother's death. I never had the chokes checked, never patterned the gun on paper; I just took it hunting. And despite the grief and horror that had come barging into my life, I shot it well.

One day in the middle of November, it seemed I couldn't miss. I was hunting with two friends, and we went to the same public area where Tori had recovered the banded woodcock. Each of us brought his springer spaniel. I had Jenny; Bob was hunting with his male, Sky, whom he had bought while on a trip to England; and Dale was following Ginger, Tori's littermate and the product of a mating between Jenny and Sky. In the morning, I killed a woodcock with the 20-gauge. A little later we were standing in a field when I heard a volley of shots some distance behind us. The others were discussing where we should hunt next, and I turned my head, and out of the tail of my eye I saw a pheasant flying toward us. It was a hen. Hens were legal game north of Interstate 80 that year, and we were a couple of miles north of that line. I waited without saying anything. The bird was high and moving fast. I squared my feet to its line of flight, swept the gun to my shoulder, gave the bird a healthy lead, and pulled the trigger for the choke barrel. The pheasant dropped like a stone. I had some complaints about ringing ears, and needed to do some apologizing. Later that morning, Jenny tracked a running pheasant for almost a hundred yards before putting the bird out of a honeysuckle thicket. A rooster, he came up cackling and curled back to my right: not a difficult shot at all.

By noon each of us had his two-bird limit of pheasants. We decided to hunt some grouse cover near Dale's house. One of the dogs chased up a grouse, a large cock that flew straight ahead between Bob and me. We both shot at the same moment. The grouse turned a somersault in midair and lodged in the top of a hawthorn. Feathers came snowing down. The dogs ran around beneath the bush, not realizing that the bird had hung up in it. The grouse had been hit hard; it was clear that Bob and I had both centered it. Both of the bird's wings and both of its legs were broken, and yet the grouse was still alive. Grouse are not usually hard to kill: sometimes a single pellet will do the job. This bird, however, sat in the thorny crown with its wings and legs akimbo, its head up, and a wild and uncompromising look in its eyes. I reached in past the thorns and drew the grouse out. With the thumb and middle finger of one hand, I encircled the bird's backbone, putting pressure on the area between the breast muscles and the spine. That is the most humane way I know of, to kill a wounded bird: its heart and lungs crushed, the creature expires quickly. After a few seconds, the grouse's head slumped to one side; its wings beat rapidly, then they fluttered, and trembled, and finally hung limp. Later that afternoon, Jenny rooted another cock grouse out of the broken top of a big red oak that had crashed down during a summer storm. That bird I killed with a snap shot, sending it tumbling down a leaf-strewn slope.

It had been a productive day, spent in the company of good friends. I had shot at five gamebirds and had hit all of them. Maybe I shot well because I didn't care whether I hit or missed. I think I get more pleasure out of retelling the story of that hunt than I felt when it was happening. Today, I realize how good it was for me to be out on the land during those bleak days. It was a balm to my soul, which I dimly realized at the time, although that did not motivate me to go hunting as often as it should have.

I don't know how many times I was afield that autumn. I was in no state to jot down notes about my outings. On some days when I entered a covert, each step seemed an obstacle to overcome. Yet when ten steps had been taken, or twenty, or a hundred, there was no sense of achievement, no sense that the next step could be accomplished any more easily than the last. Once at day's end I slipped my shotgun into its case, and when I got home I found that the gun was still loaded. I am careful to keep the muzzles of my gun directed away from people, dogs, and anything else I do not intend to shoot at: I religiously follow the rule of always treating a gun as if it were loaded, even when I know (or think I know) that it is not. Perhaps there was no precise danger in carrying around a loaded gun, since I had not pointed it at anyone. But when I opened the gun to clean it that evening, and saw the brass ends of the cartridges still in the breech, I shuddered.

As it happened, the fall of 1995 was the last autumn in many years in which we had reasonably good numbers of grouse. I did not take advantage of the situation; and of course no one could have known that bird numbers would fall so drastically. The following spring was the first of the years in which cold rains decimated the spring broods—years that followed one after another, winnowing the birds again and again. In the autumn, a scarcity of grouse (on some days, no flushes at all); a morose and distracted mind; and weather that all too often was uncomfortably warm and droughty—all conspired to rob my hunting of pleasure, and to persuade me that there were better things to do with my time.

I became involved in a new activity that, while it drew me further from hunting, ultimately helped me find the joy in life again. The year after we had summered in Iceland, my wife had gone back to that land on her own. She had searched out and bought a pair of Icelandic horses and brought them home to Pennsylvania. Nancy is also a writer, and she told the story of her quest in a beautiful memoir, *A Good Horse Has No Color.*

We kept the horses at a nearby farm while building a small barn on our own place. Nancy invited me to go riding with her. I didn't want to at first; I had never ridden and was afraid to try. As the months passed, I saw how much Nancy enjoyed riding. It didn't take me long to strike up a friendship with the horses, both of them sturdy and handsome bays, the mare a rich, dark brown and the gelding a reddish brown, like birch leaves in autumn. The horses were smart and good-natured. (Americans would call them ponies, because they stand less than fourteen hands tall: Icelanders bristle at that label, since "pony" suggests a horse that a child should ride, and these animals are simply horses with short legs: tough, strong, fast.) Under saddle, Nancy kept assuring me, Icelandic horses are sure-footed, sensible, and inclined to look out for their riders. What I needed to do, she told me, was to let my fear go, to sit loose and free and allow the animal to move beneath me: to keep out of its way. I had to remember that any fears or tensions I felt would be communicated, through my body, to the horse. In time, I screwed up my courage and decided that I, too, could learn to ride. Nancy arranged for both of us to take lessons from professional riding instructors from Iceland and Germany who were visiting in the United States. I rode the gelding, Birkir, whose name means Birch; Nancy rode her mare Gaeska, which means Kindness.

In one of her stories, Willa Cather describes a horse as "a silent companion on the empty desolate spaces, one who never failed her, and much stronger than any of us so that when he obeyed and did her will, she drew from his strength as well as her own." Birkir never failed me. He became the companion who carried me through the empty desolate spaces of my life. I would not have imagined that I would revel in galloping down a road astride a powerful animal. Riding, I soon learned, was very different from working with a hunting dog. In the human-dog relationship, the human is clearly in charge (or at least he'd better be, if he wants to end up with birds in the game pouch). The dog is a predator, a hunter, and so is the human, and both must cooperate to bring about the desired end. The horse, on the other hand, is ancestral prey. It is a flight animal that has consented to domestication. You must assert your dominance over a horse, but you can't just smack it or drag it around by the collar to make it obey. The partnership is one of a different order altogether. And at the most basic level remains the fact that every time you get on a horse's back, you place your life in the animal's care.

This is a book about hunting and not a book about horses, and I won't stray into describing the joys and challenges of riding or try to express my admittedly rudimentary understanding of the equine mind. But I will say that my bay gelding has become my close and steadfast friend. Riding competes with dog training and bird hunting, and, on a given autumn afternoon, riding may win out.

~

Caillie, however, has ways of seducing me. A lick on the hand. Sitting down next to me and leaning against my leg. Lying by the door and giving me a sidelong glance.

Then there are the guns. Shotguns are immensely sensuous objects. I own three of them, a Ruger over-and-under in 12 gauge, which I use for clays, and two game guns, side-by-sides made between the world wars in Birmingham, England, for the London-based firm W.J. Jeffery. Almost daily I get out the side-by-sides and handle them. One is a 16 bore; the other is the 20 with which I shot the banded woodcock, and shot the five birds on that memorable day with my friends. The 16 is an exquisite piece, with a lustrous walnut stock in which black figuring swirls throughout a chestnut brown background. Fine engraving covers the receiver, and almost all of the original case-hardening color graces the action's metal. The 20 gauge is a plain gun. It has the classic straight English stock and splinter forend, but the wood is bland, with little figuring. The receiver is engraved with a rather loose scroll, and some hardening color remains, although I'm doing my best to wear it off. The barrels, twenty-seven inches long, have been reblacked. The stock bears numerous scratches and nicks, dings and dents.

The 20 gauge is my everyday gun, my "bramble divider." I don't hesitate to carry it in the rain. It has been to Minnesota, and Wisconsin, and up and down and over and through these Pennsylvania hills. I have fallen with the gun on several occasions, once landing on top of it: snow-covered scree on the south face of Stone Mountain, but the barrels weren't dented, and we flushed grouse that afternoon, and I killed a brace.

The Jeffery 20 fits me perfectly. It weighs five and a half pounds, which is what a grouse-and-woodcock gun ought to weigh, at least for someone of my size and weight: five feet, nine inches, and 150 pounds. I can hold it in one hand while parting the brush with the other. I can carry it from dawn to dusk. It balances at the hinge pin and has a solid, between-the-hands heft. It is a quick gun, yet one that remains under control. The left barrel has a fair bit of choke and has killed birds, such as that high-flying hen pheasant, out to forty yards.

I do not apologize for the fact that I like guns—or at least, good guns. The smoothness of barrels and stock, and the roughness in just the right places, such as the checkering on the wrist and the forend. The shape, which is utterly correct and as devoid of superfluousness as any predatory animal. Even a gun's smells transport me: the aroma of stock polish and the tang of cleaning solution, the acrid whiff of burnt gunpowder that you get when you open the gun after firing it—all signals reminding me that life is short, and, as much as possible, one ought to enjoy it, and the very best way of enjoying life is to spend it out-of-doors.

~

I'm carrying the bramble divider when Dale and Ginger and Caillie and I leave the truck along a gravel road on state forest land. It's a Saturday, and Dale and I are both off work. We're in Huntingdon County, the next county to the south from Centre, on the side of Stone Mountain—the same mountain on which I fell with the 20 a few years back. I took my tumble on the south-facing slope; we're on the north slope today, because that is where Dale ran into several broods of grouse when cruising timber here this past summer. Dale buys standing trees for a small sawmill; he covers a lot of territory, and over the years he has located some good bird coverts for us.

It's the sixth time I've been hunting this fall. I have shot at a few woodcock and missed them. I have yet to flush a shootable grouse. I don't consider myself to be that inept of a hunter or Caillie that incompetent of a bird dog. And my coverts aren't all so old and past their prime that we should have found so few birds in them. I'm afraid it's going to be another lean year. Yet the grouse were here, Dale tells me, along the road and on the edge of this clear-cut, just two months back.

In any case, it's a grand day to be afield. There's not a cloud in the sky, which is such a deep, pure blue that it seems to glow. The mountains are aflame with color. About half of the leaves remain on the trees; we're thirty miles south of Bald Eagle Valley, and autumn here isn't quite so far along.

We stand before the huge clear-cut. Looking at the young trees that are growing on the site, I'd estimate that the cut is probably ten to twelve years old. I wish I had known of it a few years earlier, when it would have been in its prime; however, it still looks like pretty decent grouse cover. Many of the stumps have sent up sprouts: white oak, red oak, chestnut oak, with quite a few red maples mixed in, and here and there a hickory, tuliptree, or ash. A few white pines stand singly and in scattered copses among the hardwoods. Numerous black birches have seeded themselves onto the cut; the birches, which browsing deer don't find as tasty as the oaks, are shooting skyward, and in many places they have overtopped the gnawed-off oak sprouts. A lot of foresters believe that in future years black birch and red maple will come to dominate Pennsylvania's forests, particularly the mountain forests in the southern half of the state, as the oaks there die off following repeated defoliations by gypsy-moth caterpillars. (Most trees can withstand having all of their leaves eaten off in one year. But after two or more successive defoliations, the trees run out of carbohydrate stores and, without their leaves to conduct photosynthesis and to build up their energy reserves, they perish.)

In this clear-cut, the stump sprouts and the young birches are four to five inches in diameter, growing above an understory of mountain laurel, lowbush blueberry, and bracken ferns, all plants that signal an acidic soil derived from a sandstone bedrock. The soil on Stone Mountain is thin and infertile, as it is on most of the sandstone ridges in Pennsylvania's Valley and Ridge Physiographic Province. That's why the mountains remained forested while the valleys, with their richer limestone soil, were cleared for farms and towns. After the mountains were logged by private companies in the late 1800s and the early 1900s, two newly formed state agencies—the Pennsylvania Game Commission and the Department of Forests and Waters—wisely bought up the land, knowing that the trees would grow back. The forests have returned, and now state game lands and state forests preserve those wooded tracts in a region that is otherwise fairly heavily developed.

Before Dale and I start our hunt, I make Caillie hup. I lead her around at heel for a few minutes, hupping her every now and then. Dale has to scold Ginger, who wants in the worst way to get going. Finally she defies him by heading into the brush on her own. He nicks her with the electronic collar she's wearing, and she yelps and returns and grudgingly hangs around with us. Ginger is as tough-minded as Caillie is soft. Both are stubborn in the insistent, ingratiating manner typical of spaniels. Dale is a quiet, placid fellow, and I've watched Ginger take advantage of him on more than a few occasions. From a notebook entry I made after a hunt years ago: "If only I had a nickel for every time Dale told Ginger to heel, or to hup, or blew his whistle at her." I imagine that more than a few of my bird-hunting companions have thought the same while hunting with me and my dogs. In temperament, Ginger reminds me of her mother, except Ginger is even more intense than Jenny was, more independent, a difficult bitch to train and keep in check: a classic dog out of field-trial lines. (This is somewhat ironic, since I bred Jenny to a dog imported from England, which I assumed would temper the American field-trial breeding. So much for my brief career as a breeder of spaniels.)

Finally I release Caillie, and we start our hunt. Dale and Ginger angle off to the left, while I follow Caillie up a crease in the mountainside toward the right. We've gone about a hundred yards when Caillie's tail starts whipping double-time and her nose makes little slurping sounds. She leaps ahead. Quickly I maneuver myself into an opening in the brush. I set my feet, my boots toed toward where the dog is working, my hips ready to swivel in whatever direction a bird may fly. I'm also ready to hup Caillie with the whistle, or to start hot-footing it over the stones if she takes off after a running grouse.

I hear a bird stutter up. The wing noise comes from a small island of pines, and I get my gun swinging in that direction before I ever see the grouse. Suddenly the bird appears above the pines, and I catch it with a snap shot. As I take the shot, I hear a second bird flush. The grouse that I've hit falls straight down but with its head held upright, which tells me I've broken a wing and haven't killed the bird. I do not see the second grouse; it must have flown directly away from us.

Caillie runs off after the second grouse. There are two schools of thought regarding steadiness in spaniels. The first school says that a steady dog—one that hups at the flush or shot—is better able to mark the bird's fall, because it isn't dashing madly ahead; when released to retrieve, the steady dog is able to go straight to the fall. (Other disadvantages to being unsteady: the dog may bump birds that haven't been shot at, it may hurt itself by crashing into a fence or some other unseen obstruction, and it may get in the way of a shot.) The other school of thought holds that the dog sees the bird well enough even when running in, and gains an advantage because it gets on a wounded bird more quickly, preventing it from running off.

In this instance, had Caillie been steady I probably would have noticed that she was looking in the wrong direction, and could have broken her concentration on the grouse that hadn't been shot and sent her after the one that had. As it is, it takes me almost a minute to whistle her back in and get her on the trail of the wounded grouse. I suppose I could have gone looking for the bird myself, but something tells me it's a runner, and I doubt I could have found it; also I did not want to disturb the scent trail. Besides, it's the dog's job to fetch, and a good spaniel ought to be able to puzzle out a track. Although today does not look to be an auspicious one for scenting, as the ground is dry and covered with brittle leaves.

"Dead bird!" I tell Caillie, leading her to the spot where the grouse should have come down.

In this situation, Jenny would have put her nose down, found the foot scent, and worked out the trail. Caillie is more inclined to rush in the general direction of the fall and then cast about for body scent. If no scent presents itself, she soon loses interest. And she's faster than Jenny was: all too often, those long legs cause her to overrun the scent. Had I been a more diligent trainer, I would have given her extra work on running birds, such as wing-clipped pheasants. I might have used a shackled duck, its wings pinned against its body by a rubber band. You do it at night: shine a light in the dog's eyes so it can't see well, then put it on the trail of the duck, which has waddled off dragging its scent-rich bottom along on the ground. For the umpteenth time, I vow that my next spaniel will be steady. And I'll take care of all the other little details, the polishing and the final training that elevate a dog to its highest level of performance. I won't simply call it quits when the dog is mostly trained, and head for the field and start hunting.

Caillie veers off to the right; I think she's working on old scent rather than following the wounded grouse, but just to be sure, I wait. Before long I whistle her back in. "Dead bird, dead bird," I tell her. I give her another line on the grouse, but I can tell it's hopeless: she just starts hunting for another contact.

I work to hold my anger in check. Caillie hasn't really committed a sin or done anything blatantly wrong; she just hasn't done something right. I remind myself that she lacks the experience to realize what it is she needs to do in this situation.

By now Dale has come over to see if I've gotten the bird. I tell him what happened and ask him to put Ginger on the trail. We walk in the general direction that the grouse must have gone. Quickly Ginger picks up the scent. Her wagging white tail-tip disappears into the undergrowth. In a couple of minutes, back she comes. Dale takes the grouse from her and somewhat sheepishly gives it to me: missing half of its tail, and dead. Ginger can have a hard mouth. That's something she didn't inherit from her mother. Still, I'm glad to slip the broken-winged bird into my pouch, rather than leave it huddled beneath a clump of huckleberry, to feed a fox or a raccoon tonight.

Despite Caillie's lackluster fetching performance, we're off to a good start, with two birds flushed and one bird bagged in the first half hour. My first grouse of the year: its weight at the back of my vests feels reassuring. We continue up the mountain, stepping over deadfalls, crouching to pass beneath low branches. We get most of the way to the top, where the clear-cut ends at a wall of gnarled chestnut oaks. We discuss making a pass through the open woods on top, but it doesn't look like good grouse cover to either of us. So we angle back down the slope, checking out seeps and little spring runs, thickets of springy-stemmed mountain laurel and patches of blackberry. We hunt hard, and we hunt thoroughly. We stop and eat our lunches in a sunny glade amid a stand of pines just beyond where the clear-cut ends. After those first two birds, we didn't raise another grouse.

We return to the gravel road. The cover looks just as good and maybe even better on the opposite side: plenty of dead and downed trees, mainly oaks killed by the gypsy moth in the past, plus some tuliptrees that must have blown down in a recent storm. Grape tangles, witch-hazel thickets, big areas of flowering dogwood, and swatches of blackberry. I check the breeze; it's faint enough not to be a factor. We hike west about a mile along the road, with the dogs at heel, until the dense brush on our right gives way to open woods. Then we get into the cover, turn around, and start hunting toward the east, with the lowering sun at our backs: much better to have the birds staring into the sun, rather than our trying to shoot into the sun at flushing grouse.

Robins are everywhere, feeding on grapes and on the bright red fruits of the dogwoods. They take off on rushing wings, fly ahead while scolding us, settle back down, and start feeding again. They precede us, gossiping and complaining, along the bench. Dale works the slope above, and I'm about thirty yards below him, with the dogs thrashing the cover between us.

We get two more flushes, both of them in front of Dale, but he doesn't have a shot at either bird. By the time we walk tiredly out onto the road, the sun is setting. We have moved a total of four grouse since midmorning: a small fraction of the birds that Dale saw here two months earlier. We case the shotguns and load the dogs into the truck.

I'm happy to have bagged my first grouse of the season, but I'm not feeling very hopeful. My friend Carl is due to arrive tomorrow for five days of hunting in the upcoming week. I hope we find enough birds to make chasing them worthwhile.

Chapter 8

I got my first taste of bird hunting when I lived in Harrisburg in the mid-1970s. Back then, the ring-necked pheasant was the premier gamebird in the rolling fertile land around the state capital. Fresh out of college, I was working as a writer for the Pennsylvania Game Commission, and when I went hunting it was usually with Bob Bell, my immediate supervisor and the editor of *Pennsylvania Game News* magazine. Bob was a tenacious hunter, a deadly wingshot, and a generous man. He taught me much, about writing and hunting and other things as well. On his advice I bought my first good shotgun, an Ithaca 20-gauge side-by-side, a short-barreled Model 280: even then, the clean lines of a straight English-style stock gladdened my eye.

Pheasants were plentiful enough that we could usually flush them even without a dog. In some of the places where Bob and I hunted—mainly on state lands open to the public, but also on privately owned farms—we kicked ringnecks out of picked cornfields and patches of brush. Later in the season, after the fields had been hunted hard and the corn harvested, we found pheasants in the honeysuckle thickets and rose tangles of river bottoms, and there we flushed woodcock as well.

On other days, in other places, it seemed that every way we turned, there would be a new house peeking through the brush, or the sound of a car door shutting, or children's voices. In three years of living in Harrisburg, I saw too many of huntable acres become shopping centers, strip malls, and housing developments: the land bulldozed flat, streets and sewers and parking lots put in, buildings erected.

I never let myself get comfortable in Harrisburg. I rented a small apartment in a rundown neighborhood, both because it was cheap and so I wouldn't be tempted to stay. I saved every penny I could. Living in the city, I felt closed in. Around me lay a confusion of roads; along them, and because of them, development was reaching into the countryside, sprawling out farther and farther each year. It took a substantial drive through traffic-clogged suburbs to get out onto good natural land. I knew I didn't want to live in the city. Neither did I want to live in a crackerbox house in the suburbs and become a commuter committed to that twice-daily head-long rush.

When I left my job with the Game Commission, it caused my father a deal of consternation: a child of the Depression, he believed that when you had a good job, you stuck with it. But it had become clear to me that I didn't want to work in Harrisburg all my life. I headed west, and did a stint in a graduate writing program in Oregon. When that didn't pan out, I returned to the hills and fields of Centre County.

I rented a remodeled summer kitchen attached to an old stone farmhouse. After a year of trying to make a living by selling articles and short stories to magazines, I landed a job at Penn State (on the same magazine where I'm temporarily working again this year). In my spare time, I drove around the countryside ferreting out places to hunt. I started using my little Ithaca and applying some of the techniques that Bob Bell had taught me to the hunting of ruffed grouse.

I bought land in Bald Eagle Valley, both because it was affordable and because the valley, I had discovered, contained more grouse and woodcock cover than anywhere else around. I met Nancy on the job; she and I fell in love and married. I began to build our house, a stressful endeavor, since I had never before constructed anything so large, complex, and expensive.

To avoid taking out a mortgage, we proceeded in stages. We didn't mind walking around for a couple of years on plywood subfloors, or reading the cautionary text printed on the brown-paper coverings of insulation batts. If we didn't have the funds to buy drywall or hardwood flooring, we waited until we did: the last thing either of us wanted to do was to borrow thousands of dollars and then squander money paying off a loan. We didn't want to chain ourselves to monthly payments: it was part of a strategy we had worked out, to someday succeed as freelance writers.

Once we were settled into our new home, I got myself a springer. Nancy picked her out of a box full of squirming pups. We named her Bald Eagle Generator—call name, Jenny—in honor of the electric generator that we ran for an hour or so each day to power our house during the first three years we lived in it, before the other houses came marching out Mountain Road and before the utility company extended their line far enough that we could hook onto the grid. When I quit my job at Penn State in the mid-1980s, the university offered my position to Nancy. Now I had more time to spend in the forests and wetlands and game coverts. I wrote a book about training Jenny and hunting with her during her first season, and then had a second book published, on the different breeds of hunting dogs. And for six, eight, almost ten years, the coverts I had collected and gotten to know and zealously guarded remained for the most part intact.

Then the same development that had made Harrisburg an inhospitable place for me came slouching into Centre County.

∿

In a recent book called *The Bulldozer in the Countryside,* the historian Adam Rome identifies the house-building boom that followed World War II as "an environmental catastrophe on the scale of the Dust Bowl." The boom and the accompanying mass migration to the suburbs—made possible largely by the automobile—destroyed huge expanses of farmland and wildlife habitat while banishing the open space that formerly surrounded

America's cities. From 1945 to 1970, Rome writes, "Every year a territory roughly the size of Rhode Island was bulldozed for urban development." After exhausting the flat, easy-to-build-on terrain, developers found ways to exploit more environmentally sensitive sites such as hillsides, wetlands, and floodplains.

Hunters and anglers were among the first to decry this loss of land. Rome contends that urban sprawl had a certain "generative power," drawing public attention to other environmental problems, including air and water pollution and the extinction of wild species. It goaded a lot of people into action, many of whom had never fired a gun or flipped a lure. A new group of activists and a new set of grassroots organizations arose, adding their voices and political clout to those of the earlier conservationists. Politicians heard those voices of protest, and during the 1970s Congress passed the Clean Air Act, the Clean Water Act, and the Endangered Species Act. What they did not manage to turn into law was the National Land Use Policy Act, a piece of legislation that could have led to a compelling vision of sound development. The Land Use act would have provided a forum in which our society could have openly discussed the importance of preserving green space for future generations, as has been done in England, a country where the human population exists at a much greater density than in the United States. After years of debate, property rights advocates, mainly on the political right, prevented passage of the National Land Use Policy Act, a law that would have given societal and environmental values equal weight with individual property rights.

While preserving our personal freedom, we lost a tremendous opportunity to preserve the landscape. Most Americans, I believe, still have it in mind that the land is limitless, that there is always more open space lying beyond the horizon. That concept has driven our culture since the time this continent was settled. Not so in the Old World: I am thinking again of England, a place where I have traveled and hunted. There, the society as a whole realized that farmland must be protected: that a nation with a population of nearly fifty million has to feed itself using a finite number of acres. England is one of the most densely populated countries in the world. Yet through planning and zoning, people have concentrated their developments in towns and cities, and outside of those specified urbanized areas lie protected forest and agricultural land. You see a lot less strip development in England than you do in America. You see many fewer houses scattered across the landscape.

After that pivotal era when Americans passed laws to protect our air and water and wildlife—and when we deigned not to make the complex, painful decisions about which land should be built upon and which land should remain in a natural state—development really took off. By the middle of the 1990s, sprawl was consuming more land than ever: 3.2 million acres a year. And the pace of sprawl today shows no signs of slowing down.

~

When good, natural places start to dwindle—or in years when native birds are scarce—many hunters turn to preserves, commercial operations that raise pheasants and other gamebirds (although not ruffed grouse: they are too flighty to be mass produced and reared in a pen) and release them into fields where paying customers can hunt them. I like shooting preserves, because they keep land open and undeveloped. But on a free-lance writer's income I can't afford to hunt on such places. I have bought exactly one hunt, during Caillie's first season, when I felt she needed some concentrated bird work. When invited to shoot on a preserve, I will usually accept. Hunting where there is an abundance of birds is undeniably exciting. It provides good wingshooting practice and represents an excellent opportunity for training a dog. But the unnatural plenitude of game and the muted instincts of the birds leave me cold. Hunting should never be too easy. I would rather do as T. H. White described it in his memoir about living in the countryside of Britain, *England Have My Bones:* "rise with the sun, and walk all day, and earn what you kill, and be satisfied with little or nothing."

Just now, I'm working at being "satisfied with little or nothing": one grouse bagged in six outings. A total of five flushes on grouse and four on woodcock. Seven successive years of bird numbers that don't hold a candle to those of the good autumns gleaming in my mind from the past. I would like this season to be something special. I worry that it will be humdrum, or even worse.

To be sure, other small things in the coverts deliver their own satisfactions. The vibrant colors of the leaves and the pleasant lay of the land. The way the long-hoped-for rain drums on my shoulders and patters on the ground and cleans the air. The sight and sound of water flowing and succoring the land. The rich, fecund smells arising from muddy low places. Turtles trundling through the grass, the *whoosh whoosh* of a raven's wings, hawks soaring overhead in their autumn passage. Dew-covered spider webs, glistening snail trails, lichens plastered to tree bark, flowers and fungi and moss. I like the way my legs keep twitching after I've spent the day hunting, and how I fall asleep the moment my head hits the pillow.

In some of the lean years, I kept on trying: different coverts, different times of the day, different weathers—rainy, snowy, clear. Some hunters think nothing of jumping into the car and driving a hundred miles to hunt. I dislike driving, and do as little of it as I can. I hate the way that cars and roads and our reliance on fossil fuels and our insistence on being able to drive wherever and whenever we wish have changed our environment, have changed the very face of the land. I'm a homebody, I guess, and one who is just stubborn enough to want to hunt near my home, in places to which I am accustomed and of which I have an intimate knowledge— places that I hold dear. I realize now that in those impoverished seasons I would have been better off making the long drive to some other area that still held birds (although I had heard that bird numbers were down throughout much of Pennsylvania, and it is no easy task to go to some unfamiliar place and find good hunting cover there). But I kept on believing that if I persevered, if I kept pounding the coverts, I'd get my share of flushes in the end. It didn't work out that way, not in 1996, 1997, 1998, 1999, 2000, or 2001. I wonder what will happen this year in 2002.

The season is still young. And when it comes to the pursuit of ruffed grouse, I must classify myself as an optimist.

~

On Sunday, the day after my grouse hunt with Dale, Nancy and I ride our horses up the Dug Road in the morning. Afterward, we give them a good brushing and clean and oil the saddles and tack. In the afternoon I work outside, raking the fallen leaves off of our patchy, weed-infested lawn. (For me hunting, dog training, shotgun shooting, horseback riding, canoeing, bird-watching, berry-picking, wood-splitting, or just plain walking in the woods rank higher—considerably higher—than grooming grass.) Caillie lies in the sunlight on our deck, her chin settled on her crossed paws, staring at me with her imploring brown eyes. I had to command her to stay there: otherwise she would have gone coursing through the woods, trying to get between chipmunks and their burrows. I told her she'd better rest and build up her strength for the week to come.

Raking the leaves into the surrounding woods (whence the wind will probably blow them back onto the lawn, but who cares?), I wait for Carl to come driving down our lane. If, when it comes to bird hunting, I am an optimist, then Carl is an eternal, incurable optimist.

He shows up just before supper. Carl is always welcome, especially when he arrives bearing a meal (a big pot of vegetable soup for later in the week: his wife Mary made it); libation (as I do, he enjoys single-malt Scotch whisky); and dessert (a good Pennsylvania Dutchman, he has a keen sweet tooth and has brought two pies, blackberry and shoofly). I kid him about making sure we'll have plenty of Dutch health food on hand, plus our minimum daily requirements of vitamins S_1 (sugar) and S_2 (Scotch).

After supper Nancy retreats to our bedroom to read, since Carl's and my endless discussion of shotguns, ruffed grouse, shotguns, woodcock, shotguns, pheasants, and shotguns tends to bore her. Will is in his room, either doing homework or reading (both of which I approve) or playing computer games (chasing electrons around on a cathode ray tube won't do much for your intellectual development, I've told him more than once). Will is not a hunter. He's fourteen, an age when many young males in Bald Eagle Valley are pestering their fathers to buy them new rifles and shotguns and take them out hunting. I wish Will wanted to hunt, but he has never shown much of an interest in guns, and he says he has no desire to kill an animal, even a toothsome one like a grouse. He likes to eat game, everything from venison to dove to duck, and he particularly enjoys the complex taste of woodcock. But I've not pushed him to hunt. Always present in my mind is the fact that my nonhunting father never said a word to discourage me, his only son out of three who liked—one might say became fixated upon—hunting.

Carl works for the state game commission; over the years, he has risen through the agency's ranks to direct the bureau of information and education. It must be the perfect job for him, because he never tires of hunting, or talking about hunting.

It was Carl who introduced me to English guns. Over the years, I watched enviously as he bought, tried out, extolled, fell out of love with, and sold various double-barreled shotguns. Old Ithacas. A.H. Fox guns. Parkers. Winchester Model 21s. Then he acquired a Harrison & Hussey 12-bore boxlock with a London address engraved on the top rib. When I picked up that gun, a light went on in my brain. No other shotgun I had ever handled felt nearly as well-balanced. A gun is a mechanical object, to be sure; and those shotguns that are the least mechanical are, in my opinion, the purest and the most beautiful, the least obtrusive, the least apt to complicatedly interpose themselves between hunter and prey—the least likely to obscure the act of hunting. Plus, they are the most effective bird-getters I have ever had the pleasure of firing.

I got an inexpensive education watching Carl buy, trade, and sell. I had some old sporting art that had gained value, and I sold it. That money formed the basis of what I termed my "gun fund," and I began doing a little buying and selling myself. After having gone through the better part of a dozen English shotguns, I'm happy with the two W.J. Jeffery guns I now own. A fancy gun in superb condition, for admiring, handling, shooting on the clays range, and taking afield on lambent days in gentle coverts. And a "using gun" for the determined pursuit of woodcock and grouse.

After shooting English guns for almost a decade, I can understand the words of T. H. White in *England Have My Bones,* when he wrote about using a "lovely Westley Richards": "I can't describe the drive and accuracy of this gun. You feel the shot go from the shoulder and keep together all the way to the bird, as if there was an invisible but tangible line linking you to it . . . a venomous arm reaching through the air for its prey."

By now Carl has sold the Harrison & Hussey 12 bore that got us started on English side-by-sides. He is also trying to peddle a lovely, pristine Harrison & Hussey 16 bore, a gun that he swore up and down he would never sell. (I enjoy reminding him of this broken pledge.) He is now besotted with English hammer guns. Tonight he gets out his current pets: a Charles Lancaster 12 bore; a William Moore and Grey 16; and a James Woodward 16. They are the only guns he plans to hunt with in the coming week. I tell him he's becoming increasingly primitive in his choice of weapons: clearly he is following a line of devolution. At first, modern over-and-under shotguns. Then vintage English hammerless guns (they're not really hammerless; they just have their hammers tucked away inside their action bodies). Next, even more venerable hammer guns. Tomorrow it will be muzzle-loading shotguns, first flintlocks and then matchlocks. Inevitably, a bow and arrow. A thrown stick, such as a boomerang. A rock. When will it stop?

Carl chuckles at my jest and asks if I have ever had the desire to do my hunting with a hammer gun. His guns are undeniably sleek and beautiful. I like the rounded actions that many of them have, and their viperine slimness, since their actions need not be capacious enough to enclose a pair of hammers. Such firearms balance and handle extraordinarily well, especially the smaller bores: the majority of English hammer guns, 12 bores having thirty-inch barrels, would be too large and cumbersome for a fellow of my size to use with the alacrity that a grouse gun needs to display. Besides, I tell Carl, clapping down my tumbler on the table, I could not possibly be expected to keep track of a wily, devious spaniel like Caillie (the Sizzle thumps her tail from over near the woodstove), spot an even wilier and more devious grouse as it flushes from cover, thumb back a pair of hammers, and superimpose a cloud of shot on a fleeing bird. It just couldn't be done.

We carry on like this well past my usual 10 P.M. bedtime. We line up the various guns, Carl's and my own, in different comparative configurations. We pick them up, raise them to our shoulders, lower them, open and close their smoothly working actions, admire their figured stock wood, their fine engraving, their blacked steel and browned Damascus barrels. We polish them with an oil rag. We discuss the benefits of No. 8 as opposed to No. 7 ½ shot in the thick foliage typical of an early season grouse covert. What to load in the right barrel, what to follow it with in the left. Whether one should switch to a larger shot size as the season progresses, to better penetrate the birds' plumage as it grows in heavier and denser. We talk about the first covert we'll check out tomorrow.

And we wonder whether, for the first time in years, we will find good numbers of birds.

Chapter 9

In the morning a light, wet snow is falling. It falls on the shrubs and weeds and grass, melting as it lands. Clouds cover the tops of the hills and the ridges enclosing the valley to the north and south. Below the clouds, the woods are a mosaic of colors: bronze, umber, brick red, dull orange, and several shades of yellow. Contrasting with the bright colors are the rich green of pines and the darker green, almost black, of hemlocks. Carl and I stand on a grass road leading down to a large lake formed by the damming of Bald Eagle Creek. The lake mirrors the parti-colored hills. Two days ago, on Saturday, these fields would have been awash with orange, in the form of vests and hats. This is public land, fifty-nine hundred acres administered as a state park by the Pennsylvania Department of Conservation and Natural Resources. The game commission stocks the huntable areas with pheasants. The place has become such a magnet for hunters that I tend to avoid it on weekends. But today it looks as if Carl and I will have the area largely to ourselves.

With the ground damp, the scenting should be excellent. What a contrast to last autumn, when, during the whole time that Carl was up—as well as before his visit, and after it—the weather was hot, often with a desiccating breeze, making for some of the poorest scenting conditions imaginable. The sweaty, shirtsleeve weather was uncomfortable for us hunters and draining for the dog. Worse yet, there were hardly any wild birds to be found. One day, although we hunted hard through several excellent covers, Carl and I did not flush a single bird. That had never before happened to us in more than twenty years of hunting together. Even Carl, the eternal optimist and the preternaturally cheerful gunning partner, finally gave up in disgust and went home a day early.

Reaching down, I touch the hupped spaniel on the top of her small domed head. When she looks up, I raise a finger to hold her attention. Then I sweep my hand to the right, and she dives into the goldenrod and the stiff brown weeds, which are interspersed with hawthorn, gray dogwood, black-haw, autumn olive, and the ubiquitous multiflora rose. A variety of lowland trees dot the cover, including shagbark hickory, white oak, pin oak, red maple, green ash, and American elm. Hunting on a northeasterly heading, we skirt a food plot given over to a weird leafy plant with an ill-looking brownish seedhead; the plot was probably created by some overzealous land manager (maybe the manager was a pheasant hunter and didn't give a hoot about woodcock) by bulldozing off a section of formerly excellent timber-doodle feeding habitat, a low, lakeside area covered with aspen.

All good intentions aside, I doubt that this food plot will ever feed a pheasant. The birds the game commission puts out are wary of people and dogs, and they are strong fliers, but they seem to lack the survival smarts to last longer than a few weeks in the wild: at least they don't seem able to avoid predators, something I have inferred from the dozens of feather piles I've found scattered throughout the public area. Sometimes I wish this place were not stocked with pheasants, since it draws in hunters from all over the state—hunters who, if they happen to flush a woodcock, will go ahead and shoot it, even though they weren't after timberdoodles in the first place and probably won't bag enough of them to make a meal. In my opinion, with woodcock numbers dwindling, if you kill one you ought not to do it casually or incidentally.

We're desirous of finding woodcock here today: flight birds often descend on this covert in good numbers. We are on the lookout for pheasants, too, since the Saturday crowd, plus the foxes, hawks, and owls, wouldn't have gotten all the birds that were put out. And we're even hopeful for ruffed grouse, several of which Carl and I have taken here over the years. We wade through the goldenrod and high-step over rocks and fallen branches. We circle around the multiflora patches. Where I can, I follow the trails that wander through the area—trails made by deer and further beaten down by Saturday's hunters. Today Caillie is wearing a bell on her collar. I'd hate to lose track of her in here, and not just because of the mischief she might make, chasing after birds when unsupervised: Route 220 bounds the covert on the northwest, and cars and trucks go booming past. Tire whine and Jake brakes are a near-constant reminder of the road's presence, and a bit of twenty-first-century Bald Eagle Valley ambience that I could do without.

I sidestep down into a swale and clamber out on the other side. I squeeze through a band of thornapples edging an overgrown fencerow. Caillie's bell clinks on my left. Keeping my eyes on her general area, I move slowly forward; Carl, also on my left, keys off of me while paying attention to Caillie as well. I walk with the buttstock of the Jeffery 20 gauge clasped loosely between the inside of my right elbow and my side. The gun's twin muzzles point upward and ahead, floating on the edge of my vision.

Caillie's white coat flashes through the weeds. She glides, circles, lunges. A woodcock twists up from a clump of gray dogwood. It flits from left to right, against the grain for a right-handed shooter. I swing the gun strongly to build in enough forward allowance, sweeping through the bird from behind. When I shoot, the bird hesitates in mid-flight, shedding a few tan body feathers. The 'cock continues on, wings blurring. I drop the gun's buttstock off my shoulder for an instant, swivel at the waist to keep up with the fleeing woodcock, then lean into the second shot. The gun's butt finds my shoulder again, and my index finger tightens on the back trigger. The woodcock is stopped in a puff of feathers. It falls like a tossed glove.

Caillie fetches it back to me, a smallish bird, certainly a male, and probably hatched this spring. Hatched in Pennsylvania, I wonder, or is this a flight bird down from New York or New England?

Carl comes over and pushes his hearing protectors up onto his cap. "Good recovery on that second shot," he says. We look at the bird. I spread its brown wings and examine the thin, razorlike outer primaries, which cause the whistling sound a woodcock makes taking off. I look at the weak, dark-nailed feet, the fluted bill ending in a faintly toothed, prehensile tip. Carl is grinning. I'm grinning. Flakes of snow fall gently on our shoulders and hats. The belled spaniel mills at our feet, *clink-clink*. I'm not paying attention to road noise at the moment. It's good to be out here. In fact, I can't think of anything else I'd rather be doing.

We hunt onward, angling down to the corner of this section of cover, near where the lake meets another grassy road. Beyond the road the land is damp, with a small pond surrounded by cattails; on slightly higher ground lie great rude tangles of multiflora rose. The thornbushes provide a nearly impregnable escape cover for game, and some birds eat the rosehips that the shrubs produce. (Occasionally I've found rosehips in the crops of grouse; the crops of the put-and-take pheasants are generally empty.) But the thorns are a true misery to hunt through. At times I've gotten myself so hung up that it seemed I couldn't move in any direction: snagged in the elbow, snagged on the back of the knee, snagged in the neck, snagged in the belly, my hat snatched off my head, the wicked, recurved thorns gouging into my scalp. Last January I was hunting in another part of the public area; I had come because I was seeing so few grouse in their usual late-season haunts, and I was desperate to be in a place where I had at least a chance at finding birds, even if they were stocked pheasants. In the depths of one particularly joyless tangle I sliced my ear so badly that it took me twenty minutes to stanch the bleeding. I had a bandanna, which I wadded up with snow and pressed against the cut. I stood there surrounded by the wiry green and maroon canes, my shotgun opened and crooked over my arm. Caillie sat hupped and fidgeting. Fresh pheasant tracks crisscrossed the snow all around us. The blood soaked through the handkerchief and dripped onto the snow. Just then two hunters walked past, above us on the highway berm. They didn't see me, down in the puckerbrush. I heard one of them remark: "Ain't no pheasants left. Let's get outta here." Get outta here, indeed. I fished my knife out of my pocket and cut off a corner of the bandanna, soaked it in my mouth, and plastered the cloth over my ear to make a bandage. Gritting my teeth, I waded back into the thicket. In due time Caillie pushed up a hen, and I killed it; later she rousted another hen, and I got that one also.

Carl and I cross the road and spread out into the cover. In general, we know the area as Sayers, because the earth-and-stone dam that holds back Bald Eagle Creek is called the Foster Joseph Sayers Dam, in honor of a local man who won the Medal of Honor in World War II. This particular part of the shooting area Carl and I have dubbed the Forbidden City, because of the profusion of multiflora rose growing here. We pick our way forward, halting, looking ahead, trying to read the cover and avoid the worst of the thorns. It's not easy to hunt in tandem here. I end up following the dog along the right side of a particularly nasty head-high, linear clump, while Carl works the left side. I can just see his orange vest through the thorns.

I'm trying to slip past a wall of barbs when a bird flushes. I hear its wings whistling but can't see it. "Woodcock!" I yell to Carl. Then I spot the bird, curling ahead and to the right. It pitches down in a clump of gray dogwood.

"I've got him marked."

"Go ahead," Carl calls. "I can't get through here."

Woodcock will sit for an enormity of time. I don't hurry. I gather Caillie in. It must have been a near flush: she's so jazzed up that I have to heel her. We work toward the dogwoods. I release her, and she makes a wild loop out beyond where the bird came down. Using the whistle, I toll her back in. I hear her bell coming through the brush. She homes in on the scent and puts the woodcock up. It buzzes toward me, then veers to the right. I take the bird at fifteen yards. At my shot, a couple dozen red-winged blackbirds come bursting out of a clump of cattails, the males' scarlet shoulder epaulettes flashing. Caillie retrieves the woodcock, a plump hen.

When Carl and I finally get together again, we've pretty well covered the lower zone of the Forbidden City. We decide to hunt back toward the main part of the covert, working our way along just a bit higher up from where we've already been. Here the cover is thinner, with patches of knee-high grass and scattered shrubs. It's classic springer field-trial cover, and I let Caillie stretch out. She quarters to the right, and, when she gets out to twenty or so yards beyond Carl, I whistle her back across. Down the field we go, back and forth, the dog at a steady, collected run. After about a hundred yards, on a sweep toward me, Caillie buttonhooks, then lines off in a new direction.

"Pheasant," I call to Carl. "Stay with her!"

When Caillie threatens to forge ahead, I hup her with a whistle blast. We advance quickly, shotguns ready. I let her go again by blowing two faint pips. With the whistle clenched between my teeth, I'm struck by an odd thought: Could I shoot at game without having that familiar accoutrement between my jaws?

I want this to be Carl's bird, since all of the action so far has been in front of my gun. I hang back slightly and let him follow the dog. Caillie's tail whips back and forth. She slashes through the grass, slowing momentarily while figuring out the scent, then speeding up again. A hen pheasant leaps up from the cover, brown wings beating rapidly. It's a pleasure, watching Carl shoot: hammerless or hammergun, he handles his firearm smoothly and accurately. He mounts the shotgun, swings it ahead of the pheasant, and at the gun's report, the hen drops like a sack of sand.

Caillie, after trailing the running bird and obediently dropping to the whistle so that we could get within shooting range, proceeds to mess up on her mark and greatly overrun the pheasant, which lies in plain view in some low grass. In plain view, at least, for creatures who hunt mainly by using their eyes: when a bird falls stone dead and doesn't move, it releases little scent and can be tough for a dog to sniff out. I bring Caillie back with the whistle and give her a line, and finally she makes the retrieve; but when you must handle a dog excessively to get an obvious bird, some of the luster is lost. Caillie brings me the hen, and I hand it to Carl. I hold his hammergun while he pouches the pheasant.

We're on a little rise, and the view is grand. The snow has stopped, and the slate gray clouds have lifted to expose the lower hills. In their late autumn splendor, the flanks of the mountains roll away to the horizon down each side of the long valley. I am struck for the hundredth, for the thousandth time, by how beautiful and welcoming the landscape of central Pennsylvania appears. For some people, perhaps, the presence of a concrete cloverleaf, or a truck stop, or a shopping center would not diminish their enjoyment of this view. Why am I so contrary? The road in the distance hums for me a dissonant song, telling of more pavement to come, more houses, fewer natural acres, fewer grouse and woodcock and thrushes and red-winged blackbirds. This public shooting area where Carl and I are standing should remain open to hunting indefinitely. But what of the many other places that wild creatures need in which to reproduce and to find food, food to fuel their bodies for migration or to withstand the rigors of winter? What of the places that hunters and foragers and hikers and naturalists require to withstand the rigors of living in an automated, fast-paced, consumptive society?

I try to tune out the tractor-trailers rumbling past. I try not to regard this manmade lake and the surrounding public land as a sandbox for people like me. Sometimes I think too much. Better simply to hunt and not look too far into the future.

We work back the way we have come, wandering a bit to take in likely patches of cover. Sparrows scuff at the ground beneath the shrubs. A band of goldfinches in their greenish gray winter plumage sit on the tops of thistleheads, separating the seeds from the gossamer filaments: at our approach, they go skimming off in their characteristic bouncing flight. We finish out the Forbidden City without finding another pheasant or a woodcock. We cross the grassy road into the same general area where we started off in the morning. Coming through, we hunted only about a fourth of the cover, if that, so we swing upslope to cut new ground. I lose sight of Caillie but can hear her bell clinking. She's in front of Carl, so I don't whistle her back.

Carl takes three quick steps, then stops. A rooster comes boiling up out of the goldenrod, cackling loudly. At the top of the bird's rise, just as the cock levels off and gets ready to pour on the speed, Carl pulls the trigger. Later he will tell me he saw the bird running on the ground: his eyes latched onto the white neck ring. When he advanced toward the cockbird, it froze in place. Moments later, Caillie drove it into the air. She'd been on the rooster's trail, and was within ten feet when the bird lost his nerve and flushed.

On the way back to the truck, Caillie puts up another woodcock. It, too, comes up in front of Carl, who takes the bird with a single shot.

~

We eat lunch sitting in the truck, parked in a turnaround next to the crumbling concrete abutment of a now-vanished bridge that once crossed Bald Eagle Creek. A thin mist hangs above the slow-moving water. On the other side of the creek are the shabby backs of houses. A dog barks monotonously. Around us, the ground is littered with broken bottles, crumpled cans, wads of tinfoil, plastic jugs, rusting pipes, and a mattress with its stuffing hanging out. What kind of idiots—the local term is "hoofties"—would rather dump their trash here instead of carrying it to a landfill and shelling out a few bucks to dispose of it properly? We should have found a nicer place to eat lunch. I don't mind it when the mist thickens, obscuring the view.

Over sandwiches, one of us makes the observation that we have killed every bird that got up in front of us this morning. We finish our respite, get out of the truck, and start hunting. Soon the author of that earlier ill-advised remark is rewarded for his hubris when his spaniel rousts a hen pheasant, which towers up from a clump of honeysuckle, about as easy a shot as one can expect. I'm thinking woodcock and am taken completely off-balance by the pheasant. I miss the bird with the right barrel. Then I prick it with the left.

I mark the bird down near the edge of the cover, in brush that fades out into open woods. I reload my gun and take Caillie to where the bird glided in. She nearly catches the hen beneath a low shrub. The bird flaps up about four feet above the ground. It flies on for maybe thirty yards, with Caillie in hot pursuit, then drops down again. If I had steadied my spaniel, I might have been able to shoot. But I couldn't drop the hammer since the dog was running along just behind the bird. Carl sees the hen land and start legging it off through the briars, but he can't get off a shot either, since he doesn't know exactly where the dog is. Despite being right on the pheasant's tail, and even with the excellent scenting conditions, Caillie fails to work out the line. We look for the hen for a long time. We beat all through the cover. Time and again I tell Caillie "Dead bird!", hoping she'll concentrate on matters at hand and work the trail out. Finally I decide that the bird just put its head down and ran: I doubt if it's within several hundred yards by now. Even though this is a stocked bird, and even though such things happen in hunting, I feel terrible. I don't know if I should be angrier at myself, for missing the easy shot, or at Caillie, for failing to stick to the trail and recover the cripple. A black mark against both of us—but mainly against me, for doing a slipshod job of training my dog. Those little piles of pheasant feathers scattered throughout the shooting area, it occurs to me now, could easily be the result of such incompetence as my spaniel and I have just shown.

Still worked up and reproaching myself, I shoot behind on a woodcock that Caillie flushes. The woodcock flies into the gathering fog. Gone. Then, oddity of oddities, Carl puts up a woodcock himself and misses it with two shots. Later he flushes another, and misses that one also.

Despite our lousy shooting, we're coming to realize that we are in a very nice woodcock covert. It's a new one for us: a friend of Carl's, who lives in southern Pennsylvania but occasionally hunts in Centre County, had generously told him we might find woodcock in this spot, an area of old fields grown up in brush interspersed with some taller trees. As the fog continues to thicken, we hunt in a westerly direction. Although we find a few of the greenish white splashings that are fresh woodcock droppings, we don't raise any more birds. At one point, Carl startles a big doe—she leaps out of her bed in the high weeds and comes sprinting toward me. I freeze, figuring that a deer ought to be coordinated enough not to run smack into a stationary object. Fortunately, she swerves and breezes on past, missing me by a couple of yards.

Sounds are muted in here. Somebody is hammering in nails—somewhere. A dog barks, not far off. After a while we hear a car driving past us on the left. That seems odd, since the creek ought to be on our left. I get out my compass and the topographic map. After orienting the map to the compass, I conclude that we've been walking in a circle, and the big covert that we thought we had discovered turns out to be a bit smaller than we'd imagined. We hunt onward, and soon we complete our loop and spot the truck parked in the turnaround.

We're both tired, but, rather than get in the truck and head for home, we decide to hunt north along the Bald Eagle, in a stand of timber with an undergrowth of blackberry, goldenrod, and ferns. I keep hoping that the pheasant I wounded ran in here, and that Caillie will find her. But we don't pick up the hen, and we don't flush any more woodcock, either.

Chapter 10

After my mother died, I was moved to do some community service in her memory. She had served on the borough planning commission in State College, the town where she had lived for almost fifty years. It had been a good place to raise a family, a good place for me and my brothers to grow up. My father was a botany professor at Penn State; he died of a heart attack in 1986, two years into his retirement. Following his death, perhaps as a way of lifting herself up out of her grief, my mother volunteered for the planning commission. She had gotten a great deal of satisfaction from it, I could tell. She liked working with people and trying to keep the town a pleasant place in which to live.

The knock on State College had always been that it was hard to get to. The town was in the center of the state, guarded by mountains, which, since the days of wagons and railroads, had formed a barrier to easy, direct travel. Local business people had been talking of new and better roads for decades, and although I figured those roads eventually would arrive, I was unprepared for how quickly they came. The university administration wanted the roads. They had built a research and technology center and believed that a better transportation network would aid that endeavor. They put up a huge events arena and wished to fill it for shows: everything from rock concerts to circuses to professional wrestling. (Which made me wonder: Is that what a university should be about?) They added onto the school's football stadium again and again: new roads would let fans get to Penn State from all over the East.

A decade earlier, following a political redistricting, a politician from a neighboring county had become the U.S. representative for the part of Centre County that includes State College and Penn State. The politician chaired the House Committee on Transportation and Infrastructure. The road-building industry, the trucking industry, and the billboard industry contributed heavily to his reelection campaigns; and since the politician generally ran unopposed, he used his campaign funds to travel widely and luxuriously. Did the university court this scalawag? I don't know. Maybe it was only another in a long list of pork-barrel projects he had secured for his district, another payoff for the firms that kept funneling money to him.

The politician wrote into law the creation of Interstate 99.

The highway drew a great deal of criticism. The politician had worked it so that an earlier segment of the road ended near a relative's car dealership. Had the standard interstate numbering system been followed, the road's official designation would have been a more prosaic I-576 or I-776 or I-976, because at its southern end it branched off from Interstate 76, the Pennsylvania Turnpike (the interchange, at a place called Breezewood, is a wasteland of motels and gas stations and fast-food franchises). As well as specifying the highway's numerical identity, the politician somehow got the road named for himself. At times I fantasized about destroying the green-and-white signs proclaiming his name, standing along earlier-completed parts of the interstate.

Interstate 99 has appeared on a list of "The Fifty Most Wasteful Roads in America." The average daily number of vehicles on U.S. Route 220—the road running through Bald Eagle Valley, the one that I-99 will replace—was 8,400 per day, which is below the Federal Highway Administration's standard of 10,000 vehicles per day needed to justify a four-lane highway. Over time, the estimated cost of our local section of I-99 has risen from $120 million to $454 million to $750 million, with the federal government—

or, rather, the taxpayers of the United States—paying 80 percent. The U.S. Environmental Protection Agency, the U.S. Fish and Wildlife Service, and the Pennsylvania Game Commission opposed the alignment of the road, which the state department of transportation placed on the side of Bald Eagle Mountain, where it will fragment forests and where it has a greater potential for destroying wetlands and threatening aquifers: a much less damaging route would have sited the road on the valley floor on top of the existing U.S. 220.

It was obvious to me that a road like I-99 would attract traffic, including many tractor-trailers. The new highway might relieve congestion for a while, but the development that it would spawn would lead to more and worse traffic in the future.

Nancy and Will and I live in a municipality called Worth Township. As work on I-99 got underway, the township surveyed its citizens about what they wanted the area to be like in ten, twenty, thirty years. The great majority of the residents who answered the survey wanted the township to stay as rural and undeveloped as possible. Interstate 99 would include an interchange where it crossed U.S. Route 322 north of Port Matilda, about four miles from our home. The two U.S. highways, 322 and 220, run concurrently through Port Matilda, a town of six hundred people. Its buildings shake from the vibrations of passing trucks, and the air is fugged with diesel fumes; the houses are covered with road grime. Port Matilda is surrounded by Worth Township, with eight hundred residents. The I-99 interchange would be in Worth Township.

Soon we learned that one new interstate was not all we would need to contend with. The politician who had created I-99 specified the building of another large, expensive road. With a couple of paragraphs attached as a rider to a different bill, he designated a four-lane, limited-access highway, called Corridor O, to replace the existing U.S. Route 322. Corridor O would link I-99 with I-80, which runs east-to-west across northern Pennsylvania.

Interstate interchanges are prime spots for development, especially in areas already growing on their own. The meeting of two interstates, with an accompanying interchange, almost guarantees rapid sprawl. After Corridor O was legislated, I attended a meeting convened by our township supervisors. At the meeting, county planning officials explained to the public where the new roads would go and warned of the development they could bring: a picture of Breezewood sprang into my mind. Four miles from my house. From what was said at the meeting, it seemed that the only tool available to manage growth, to keep it from overwhelming the landscape and destroying the rural quality of the township, was zoning. With zoning in place, proposed developments—housing, motels, truck stops, fuel depots, factories, landfills (Pennsylvania annually accepts thousands of tons of trash from neighboring states)—could take place only in areas set aside specifically for those uses. Projects would be reviewed for their impacts on the environment and on preexisting development. In theory, a carefully written zoning ordinance could blunt some of the negative impacts of sprawl. It could limit the size and number of billboards and overhead lights. It could keep development from occurring haphazardly, with shopping centers next to houses next to car lots next to schools next to strip joints (actually there was one of those tawdry establishments already in the area, on Bald Eagle Mountain at Skytop). Through its built-in process of review and consideration, zoning could also work to slow the pace of development.

Remembering my mother and her service to her community, I wrote down my name on a list of volunteers. The supervisors asked seven of us to form a planning commission; ultimately, I was elected chairman. The township hired a consultant to help us write a comprehensive plan, the first step toward a zoning ordinance. The planning commission met twice monthly for more than a year in developing the plan, which described the township—its soils, floodplains, farmland, and forests, the existing road network and housing stock and businesses, the new roads, and the areas where growth would most likely occur. The report noted that the citizens of Worth Township wanted the area to remain rural. When we presented our plan at a public meeting, it was met with approval.

Then came the hard part: putting lines on the map, setting up the zones where different kinds of development should take place. We sought input from citizens, but few were interested in working with us. We began to hear rumblings that certain people did not want to have restrictions placed on what they could do with their land. That sounded reasonable, but we hoped we could come together as a community and make decisions that we could all live with, decisions that would protect the value of the homes we had made, decisions that would prevent Worth Township from drowning in development.

A citizens' group formed in opposition to zoning. Their leader had married into a family who owned land near the interchange. A genial, well-liked man who was active in Little League baseball, he worked in a local building supply store, where he saw many people daily. He and others in his group began spreading rumors: If zoning gets passed, you won't be able to deed land to your children. You won't be allowed to hunt, or cut firewood on your land, or fix up your house. When a planning commission member asked the opposition leader why he was spreading such outright lies, the man grinned and said: "It gets results."

People began flooding our meetings. Angry people, who did not want to listen when we tried to explain how zoning really worked and what it could do to protect the township and preserve property values. Suspicious people, who refused to cooperate in coming up with an ordinance that would not unduly limit how landowners could develop their properties while also maintaining the township's rural character. We invited the leader of the anti-zoning group to work on the planning commission with us; he demurred. The meetings became increasingly heated. We found it hard to move forward in crafting an ordinance. One night a man suggested I step outside the fire hall and settle things once and for all. Later, this same fellow opined that we should all be shot. A woman showed up, redolent of alcohol, and berated us. Lots of other people, presumably sober, also yelled at us. People called us the "zoners." They claimed the planning commission was made up of outsiders, newcomers trying to take over the township; in fact, one of our members lived on a farm that had been in his family for generations. I myself had been born less than twenty miles away and had resided in the township for over fifteen years. By no means did all of the people rise up against us: a father and son, respected landowners who ran the only remaining dairy farm in the township, both declared that they favored zoning. But many other people who supported a zoning ordinance were intimidated by those who opposed it.

Before we could finish drafting an ordinance, two of the three supervisors who had established the planning commission moved away from the township. In the next election, voters chose opponents of zoning to fill their seats; one of the new supervisors was the opposition group's leader. When, after three years of work, we finally presented an ordinance to the supervisors, they rejected it out of hand. By that time I was simply glad to be finished with the wrangling. Soon after, I resigned from the planning commission.

I had come to see zoning as no more than a rearguard battle, a delaying action in a war that had already been lost. It was lost in the 1970s, when Congress failed to pass the National Land Use Policy Act. It was lost when Penn State decided it needed to grow. It was lost when the road-building politician absorbed Centre County into his district. It may even have been lost when we as a society embraced the automobile as the primary means of getting around in our environment. After quitting the planning commission, I asked myself whether, knowing the outcome, I would work to implement zoning again. I'm not a glutton for punishment, and I don't enjoy being vilified or asked to step outside to get pounded. No, I would not take on such a thankless task. But I'm glad I did it once. I learned a great deal—about the workings of local government, the shortcomings of the planning process as it exists in Pennsylvania today, and the changes that are coming to Centre County. I learned what many of the people I lived among were really like.

One day while buying gas in Port Matilda, I encountered a man who had done some excavating work for us when we'd cleared our horse pasture. He had a young springer spaniel in the cab of his truck. He told me he was looking forward to training the puppy and using it to hunt grouse and pheasants. He was a longtime resident of Bald Eagle Valley; he lived just across the line in the next township.

He asked if I planned on doing much grouse hunting in the fall. And he told me, almost as an afterthought, and with a light laugh, that he didn't know too many landowners in Worth Township who would want Chuck Fergus, the zoning guy, hunting on their land.

I knew then that I would leave Bald Eagle Valley.

Chapter 11

Yesterday in the thick and thorny coverts at the public hunting area, Carl carried his Charles Lancaster 12 bore. The gun has beautifully fashioned Damascus barrels, with a glossy brown finish that lets the pattern of the intertwined steel and iron show through as a series of repeating silvery rosettes. The barrels are thirty inches long. The gun weighs six pounds, six ounces, and is so well balanced that it feels lighter than that. It's not a pristine piece—scratches and scars cover the stock, the checkering is worn nearly flat, and the action's steel has been abraded to a soft silvery color. Sitting in the living room that evening, bone tired and well fed, the shotguns cleaned, the game dressed and hanging in the shed, we fell to speculating on where the Lancaster had been and what it had done.

Carl had bought the gun over the telephone from a seller in England. When the Lancaster arrived, there was a piece of paper tucked into its leather case, a handwritten note stating that the gun was one of a pair owned until 1939 by a family with the surname Wigram. The note said that the original owner had been equerry to King George V. An equerry is a personal attendant to the British royal household. Through an internet search, Carl had learned that a Colonel Sir Clive Wigram served as King George's private secretary from 1911 to 1933. He was at the monarch's bedside when the king died in 1936. If the scrap of paper were to be believed, this was his gun.

King George frequently shot with the Lords Ripon and Walsingham, famously adept wingshots during the era of the immense driven bird shoots in Britain, during the Edwardian period at the end of the nineteenth century and the beginning of the twentieth century. It seemed probable to Carl and me, as each of us sat nursing a Scotch, that the Lancaster had been used during those historic occasions—those rather bizarre and excessive social events, when hundreds of birds, mainly pheasants, were driven past the waiting guns of the nobility and their guests.

I set down my glass and picked up the Lancaster. A back-action sidelock, it opens through the agency of a side lever. The hammers are gracefully shaped, and when pulled back to full cock, they disappear beneath the line of sight along the top rib. The body of the gun is pleasingly rounded, and a horn buttplate caps the end of a well-figured French walnut stock. The gun just feels right—solid between the hands, substantial without being clunky, easy to move in any direction.

The top rib of the shotgun is engraved with the maker's name and address: Charles Lancaster, 151 New Bond Street, London. Lancaster was a highly respected gunmaking firm, only somewhat less renowned than such houses as Purdey, Boss, Woodward, and Holland & Holland. The barrels on Carl's gun are stamped CL, which may mean that the second Charles Lancaster, who succeeded his father in the family business, overseeing it from 1845 until his death in 1878, himself had made the barrels. The Lancasters, father and son, were famous for the quality of their barrel work and often were commissioned by more prestigious firms to make barrels for their guns. The Lancaster's serial number, 6016, suggests that it was built around 1888; at that point, the company had been taken over by Henry Alfred Alexander Thorn, a pupil of the second Charles Lancaster. Perhaps the pupil had selected barrels made by the master, which had been set aside in stock, and used them in fashioning Sir Clive Wigram's gun.

Making shotgun barrels out of Damascus steel was an incredibly labor-intensive task. Some eighteen pounds of prepared gunmetal were required to weld a pair of 12-gauge barrels, which, when finished, weighed around three and a half pounds. It was all hand and eye work. I've heard that it took three men two and a half hours to make one rough tube. First, alternating strips of iron and steel were laid one on top of the other and, in a forge, welded into a bar. The steel often was scrap from carriage springs or the cutlery industry. For the iron component, barrel forgers favored low-carbon Swedish iron, from the recycled stubs of horseshoe nails. According to *The Gun and Its Development*, by W. W. Greener, best-quality Damascus contained more than 60 percent steel.

The multilayered bimetal sandwich was rolled out into square rods about four feet long and 3/8 of an inch by 7/16 of an inch. Each rod was heated and twisted under manual or steam power until it resembled a screw. Peter Hawker, in his book *Guns and Shooting*, likens this twisting to "wringing cloths when wet." The twisting compacted the rod to some three feet in length, with approximately eight twists to the inch. The barrel forger took three such rods and welded them side by side to form a flat strip or ribbon. "It is not usual to use more than three rods," writes Greener. "Fine Damascus barrels, as manufactured by the Belgians, are occasionally made from four or six rods together, but three are sufficient to give a very fine figure."

The ribbon was heated, coiled around a mandrel, and forged into a barrel through hammering. Greener describes the process: "Three men are required—one to hold and turn the coil upon [a] grooved anvil, and two to strike. The foreman, or the one who holds the coil, has also a small hammer with which he strikes the coil, to show the others in which place to strike." The barrel-in-progress was also "jumped": stood upright on the anvil and dealt a sharp endwise wallop to fuse the coil into a tube.

Around the end of the nineteenth century, Damascus was supplanted by the technique of boring a hole through a cast steel bar. Fluid steel, as it was called, was stronger and harder than Damascus, and less likely to dent. The general belief was that steel better resisted the pressures generated by the new smokeless nitro gunpowder that was gradually replacing the black powder of the Damascus era. New steel-making techniques yielded stock without the slag inclusions and air pockets that had plagued earlier products. And gunmakers developed machines that could accurately bore out the hard steel cylinders. Damascus barrels continued to be used for English shotguns for some time after World War I, although actual production of the barrels had probably ceased by the first decade of the twentieth century.

I rested Carl's Lancaster across my legs and looked at the intricate figuring in its barrels. So much history and beauty were contained in an object that still could be used effectively in the field. I ran my hands lightly over the walnut stock. At some point the shotgun had become somebody's rough-shooting gun: it shows unmistakable signs of having been dragged through the British equivalent of multiflora rose and greenbrier. Among his hammerguns, the Lancaster is Carl's bramble divider. Carl and I wondered aloud about the game the gun may have taken—hare, partridge, pheasant, red grouse, European woodcock—and about the days afield in which the Lancaster served Sir Clive and his successors.

"A piece of artistic hand-craftsmanship" was how the English writer Gough Thomas described one of his shotguns, adding, "Its ingenious mechanism gives me much joy to contemplate and care for—so does the patina of its beautiful wood and engraved metal." For Thomas, who could wax more than eloquent when it came to firearms and shooting, a shotgun became an "intimate, personal weapon, the proved companion in field and flood, through whose instrumentality I have known many high moments, when, for a space, blood has been transmuted into ichor, and weariness, hunger, and disappointment have been utterly forgotten."

~

On the morrow I am carrying my own intimate, personal weapon— the far humbler tool, the undecorated but shapely and effective 20-bore Jeffery—when, in the depths of the covert Carl and I call Pufferbelly, down where the creek slips past like gray-green glass, a grouse flushes from the hawthorns.

Hunters not familiar with spaniels may imagine that the dog, set down in game cover, simply bustles about until it startles a bird into flight. What a spaniel is supposed to do is to find foot or body scent, work out the trail, and home in on the bird that is releasing the scent and give it no option beyond immediately taking flight. We had just arrived at stage one in the process—Caillie's nose to the ground, her tail given over to its speed-wagging mode—when the grouse came thundering up. But thanks to the warning she'd given me, I was alert, and quickly swept the shotgun toward the bird.

Some of the birds you flush imprint themselves indelibly on the mind, and this grouse is one of them. It's a cock, clearly identifiable by its large size, the long and broad tail, and the prominent black shoulder ruffs. As the grouse powers upward, I can see the head crest held erect, the button-black eye regarding me coldly, even (maybe I'm imagining this, but I don't think so) the tiny blush of pale red skin in the zone above the eye. I have only a moment in which to shoot: the instant when the grouse clears the hawthorns and before it peels downstream, back into the thick brush. It's a ten-yard chance, maybe more like eight, a distance at which a charge of shot can rip a bird to shreds. The thing I do is shoot the grouse in the head.

Bang, and the grouse is on the ground, thrashing its wings convulsively as a head-shot bird will do.

Caillie makes the unnecessary retrieve, and I have the grouse in hand. It's warm and loose, shaking out the last of its life. This bird did not want to die, and I killed it. I know that I don't want to die. But when I go, I don't think I'd mind flashing out of this world in a like manner: headfirst off a galloping horse after I've achieved the ripe old age of, let us say, eighty-eight. Well, make it ninety. Although, of course, we cannot generally choose the time or the manner of our death.

I meet up with Carl beneath the aspens with their green-gold bark, where beaver-nipped sprouts jut up from the ground like sharpened stakes, and muddy trails show where the rodents have dragged the cut stems down to Bald Eagle Creek. I show Carl the grouse, a mature bird in its prime. He takes my shotgun while I pouch the bird, still barely quivering.

Today Carl is hunting with a different gun than yesterday, and, while he's holding onto my Jeffery, I put out my hand for his hammergun. It's a Woodward, one of the finest names in English gunmaking. The Woodward is a 16 bore. Carl bought it this past summer, and today is the first time he has hunted upland birds with it. Pufferbelly is the second covert we have visited this morning. Earlier, at the Jay Place, one of our oldest and most favored coverts, Carl killed a brace of woodcock with the gun.

The Woodward was made in 1877; Carl learned this by comparing its serial number, 3553, with data presented in a book, *Game Guns and Rifles*, by the English writer Richard Akehurst. The gun has a strikingly beautiful walnut stock with a straight-hand grip. The scroll engraved on the metal surfaces is lovely and fine. The gun is of the bar-in-wood design, with island locks, which means that the lockplates are completely surrounded by the stock wood, requiring a most exacting inletting. Carl was able to afford the Woodward because it is not in entirely original condition. The gun has been sleeved: its Damascus barrels, probably damaged by corrosion from black powder, have been replaced with modern steel barrels welded onto the original breech ends, the whole assembly then reblacked. The sleeving and the blacking jobs were nicely done; it's almost impossible to pick out where the Damascus ends and the fluid steel begins. The replacement barrels have also been worked down properly, so that the gun is light—"six pounds, just," is how the seller would have described it—and it balances as it ought to, slightly ahead of the hinge pin. Like the Lancaster, the Woodward is a lively, quick piece.

I swap guns with Carl again and get back my Jeffery, which, as they say, is "good enough for who it's for." My blood may not quite have become transmuted into ichor, but I am more than happy to have used the Jeffery in bagging this grouse—because I'm always happy to connect with a grouse, and because I'm not shooting particularly well this morning (a continuation of the sloppy work I made at the end of yesterday) and I hope this bird will put me back in the groove. In the Jay Place, I missed a woodcock and then a grouse. The woodcock was an easy enough bird. Caillie flushed it, and it towered up through the sparse, twisted tops of a clump of locust trees. Overanxious, I failed to cheek the gun properly, which sent my shot above the mark. The grouse was a more sporting chance: Caillie drove it out of a grape tangle, and I put my pattern flush onto a leafy red maple just as the bird flew behind it—a long shot, about thirty yards, and I knew the pellets didn't penetrate the foliage and connect because I took a couple of quick steps to get to one side of the screening vegetation and watched as the grouse barreled away, beyond range for a second shot, in apparent perfect health.

No complaints about the dog work. I wish the shooter had been more attentive; although sometimes the best way to break a string of misses is to be rather less attentive, or at least less concerned about what you may be doing wrong. The grouse I have just killed flushed so quickly and offered such a brief window of opportunity that I didn't need to think about it much: I just swept the gun muzzles through the front end of the bird and pulled the trigger.

We continue our tour of Pufferbelly. The sky, which was clear this morning when we started off at the Jay Place, has become, without my noticing it until now, an overall monochromatic gray. The trees glow in the suffused light. The aspens still keep a few patches of twinkling gold leaves, and the swamp maples look like beasts with patchy orange-and-red pelts. The green boughs of the pines are flecked here and there with old tan needles that will soon fall off and drift to the ground.

Pufferbelly has been a productive covert over the years. We have killed many woodcock within its bounds, and more than a few grouse, and even the occasional stocked pheasant. Once Carl bagged a turkey gobbler here. Unfortunately, I don't hold out much hope for Pufferbelly. On one side of the covert, across the creek, lies Route 220. On the other side, upslope, stretches a vast clear-cut, where every tree has been removed and hauled away or burnt to make room for the new road. At the moment, in a field between Route 220 and the creek, machines are working on an artificial wetland to replace other wetlands that the new highway will destroy. The term is "mitigation": the concept is that you "mitigate" or make up for the destruction of a certain number of acres of diverse, complex, and vital wetlands by creating a corresponding number of acres of semifunctional wet places. As I move ahead through Pufferbelly, I can hear the rhythmic pounding of some device of construction, perhaps a drilling rig; the pulsing, automated beeping sound produced by machines while backing up; and the muted roaring of graders and dump trucks going about their tasks. Background to all of that racket is the *shoosh* and mutter of passing cars and trucks.

When I-99 is finished, Pufferbelly will lie between the interstate and old Route 220. If there are still grouse and woodcock in here, which I somehow doubt, how will a hunter hear a bird flush, with the two roads droning, one in each ear?

A woodcock gets up in front of me. Caillie wasn't birdy—probably the wind wasn't right—and, distracted by my glum thoughts, I miss another bird I should have taken. Carl isn't in a position to shoot: I can see his orange vest winking behind some crabapples. I shot behind the woodcock, which now twists to the left, crosses the railroad tracks, lifts above another band of cover, speeds across the powerline right-of-way, and, continuing up the slope, disappears into the strip of woods between Pufferbelly and the big clear-cut.

$\sim$

Back in the truck, we pull out onto 220 and drive past the wetland under construction, a low spot that is being carefully graded and surrounded with a two-foot-high earthen berm that presumably will hold water. I reflect on the fact that I've never before seen a perfectly rectangular swamp, marsh, or bog. I hope that whatever they plant in there will offer food and cover to some kind of wildlife—maybe mallard ducks, which can put up with considerable noise and human interference; I can't imagine wood ducks feeding or nesting that close to a road. It's possible that amphibians will breed in the pools, but with the wetland right next to the highway, it seems doubtful that many salamanders or frogs or toads will be able to disperse into the surrounding terrain. I wonder if this place will become what is sometimes called a "sink"—a zone where animal life is extinguished rather than replenished.

We drive to Port Matilda and park near the American Legion building. We walk past an olive-drab army tank that serves as a monument, and past the tan grass of the baseball field, summertime home of the Port Matilda Porters. The Ballfield Covert commences a few yards beyond the field. It is an expanse of old fields that a lot of my bird-hunting acquaintances know about and visit in season; for some reason, the place hasn't become so overgrown with trees that woodcock don't alight there anymore. Gray dogwood, thornapples, crabapples, and goldenrod abound. The Ballfield Covert is a good place to find flight birds, and we haven't gone far before a woodcock flushes at Carl's feet.

Carl is a well-built, erect-standing man, a solid six-footer. His long-barreled shotguns fit him well. When shooting, he is unhurried, yet prompt. He possesses excellent vision: he sees his birds clearly, which confers a huge advantage to a shooter. Carl brings up the Woodward, thumbing back the hammers. He doesn't jerk the gun up; he simply raises it. His shooting style, although fluid, is also somewhat studied, and he will some-times shoulder the gun and track a bird, then swing ahead of it for a prescribed distance before pulling the trigger: not the point-and-shoot Churchill method that I use, but something a bit more rational. And effective: Carl shoots a lot of clays courses in the summer, he polishes his skills on doves in September, and come October and November he is ready to kill woodcock and grouse.

The shot sounds, and the woodcock falls into a small opening. I whis-tle for Caillie to hup; she isn't needed for this retrieve. Carl opens the gun's action, walks to the fallen bird, picks it up, and holds it out for me to see. A grin lights up his face. The Woodward 16 has just accounted for its first limit of American woodcock.

We resume, heading west, away from the ballfield. Carl flushes another woodcock, and another. He doesn't shoot the birds, since he has already limited out: one bird at the Ballfield, added to the two he took earlier at the Jay Place; now he is hoping for a grouse. Both of the woodcock that he flushed fly on ahead; maybe we'll pick them up farther into the covert, maybe not. We cross over to the south side of the railroad tracks, where the cover is thicker and looks somewhat more promising for grouse: scattered thornapples, phalanxes of crabapples, and small stands of hop-hornbeam trees with their dangling fruits that look like tiny papery pine cones. The "cones" are composed of a dozen or so bladderlike bracts, each holding a single nutlet. Grouse eat the nutlets in autumn, and they feed on the trees' buds and on the unopened, immature male catkins during winter.

Pollen from crowsfoot, it's a dainty species of ground pine, powders my boots yellow. I bend to pass beneath a crabapple, its hoary, twisted branches armed with spurs. I notice that Caillie is working scent. She's out there a ways, and I hup her and move up quickly. "Go ahead," I whisper to her, and she slips forward, darting beneath a dogwood. Out comes a grouse. The bird is screened by vegetation. It flies from right to left. My shot is behind the bird, but I don't feel too bad about missing what is a very tough shot. When my gun goes off, I hear another bird flush, off to my left. And another. Carl yells "Grouse!" but doesn't get off a shot.

I hup the spaniel and quickly reload. I loose Caillie again, casting her out to the left. She hunts in that direction, then turns and bends back across in front.

After we hunt for about twenty yards, she flushes another grouse. It flies through the brush in front of me. The bird makes a mistake: it banks to the right, heading for the cover on the other side of the railroad tracks. As it flashes into the opening, I shoot. The grouse falls onto the gravel just beyond the far rail. It lies there with its creamy gold-barred belly pointed at the sky. A cloud of down and feathers goes drifting.

We end the day thus, each with a limit of birds: Carl with three wood-cock, and I with a brace of grouse. We walk back down the tracks, headed toward Port Matilda in the drab light. A good afternoon in the Bald Eagle Valley. For a moment, with birds flushing on either hand, it seemed as if the old days were back again.

I don't know who owns the Ballfield Covert, and I've never seen any posters along its perimeter warning people away. Zoner or not, I have never been kicked off of this lovely, disheveled, grouse-and-woodcock-friendly portion of Worth Township.

Chapter 12

On Wednesday morning we go back to the public hunting area and park again at the junk-strewn turnaround next to Bald Eagle Creek. We're set to enter the covert where we did so much missing of game on Monday afternoon, where we got lost and walked, all unaware, in a circle. Last evening, celebrating our day's bag of woodcock and grouse with a wee dram, we hung a name on this covert: Endless Circle. We figured a hunter might get going in there, and trek around in pursuit of shadowy, immortal woodcock that would never fall to the gun. Abandoned by his dog, the hunter would finally starve, and his skeleton would be found at a later date, perhaps with a small black whistle between his jaws.

It's an easy enough place in which to lose oneself, especially on a murky day when the mountains hide behind clouds and sounds echo dully. The flat bottomland was a farming area before the U.S. Army Corps of Engineers condemned it in the 1960s, demolished the farms, built the dam, and backed up the creek. Carl and I load our shotguns and enter the spotty woods and the overgrown fields that comprise the Endless Circle. Pale glistening fungi grow from the wet black trunks of elm and wild cherry trees. Smells of mud and creek water rise. The Bald Eagle murmurs past.

In the fog we hunt slowly, tentatively, quietly. Caillie seems to have gotten into a rhythm. After two days of hunting, she's tired enough to willingly work in close. She looks at me, glancing back over her shoulder every so often. I need to use the whistle only a little, which seems to suit the mood of the day and certainly must be more enjoyable for Carl.

I had suggested we hunt up high this morning, out of the fog, trying an upland covert for grouse. But Carl likes to concentrate on woodcock when the birds are in. I wouldn't say we're in the middle of a wave of flight birds, but we're certainly moving enough woodcock to make hunting them worthwhile.

I stop next to a mushroom growing from a wound in a small elm. I like to forage while I hunt. Often I'll carry home wild edibles in my game pouch: a hen of the woods (that's a mushroom as well as a female grouse), butternuts, hickory nuts, chestnuts, pears and apples from some long-dead farmer's orchard. This mushroom is *Pleurotus ostreatus,* the oyster mushroom. A tasty edible variety, meaty and slightly sweet, it would be excellent sauteed in butter and reheated in cream, served as a complement to woodcock. Unfortunately, all of the specimens here are too high on the trees for picking.

There's a certain amount of suspense attendant upon entering a woodcock covert on a November morning. Will the birds be in? Some fresh gluey droppings suggest that woodcock may in fact be present. We have gone about a hundred yards when Caillie makes game and then quickly flushes a bird. The woodcock is a low flier that does not offer a shot. I mark it down and work Caillie toward the spot. She flushes the bird again, giving me a reasonable chance, and I pull the trigger but fail to connect.

Carl kicks up a bird. In the fog, the woodcock looks like a big, fast-flying moth. Carl kills it. A scant five minutes later he flushes and shoots another woodcock, and suddenly he has taken a brace. When he kicks out a third, he raises his gun to it—he's carrying the Lancaster—but lets the bird go without shooting: apparently he figures it's on course to fly past me. That is a kind thing for him to do (also, he probably doesn't want to end his gunning by taking his limit so quickly), but it takes me off balance: suddenly I'm confronted with a crossing shot at thirty yards, complicated by the bird's stunting between trees, and I miss the 'cock with the right barrel and then the left. I'm a lot more comfortable with the sudden, close-in shots than I am with the longer ones where a swing-forward lead is needed. In all honesty, I'm no great shakes with a scattergun. The English writer T. H. White was once labeled an "indifferent shot," and I could probably be placed in the same category. However, I am not at all indifferent toward the game at which I shoot. I open the Jeffery, pocket the empties, tip my hat to Carl. With a smile I salute the now-vanished woodcock: long may it live, or at least until we catch up to it again.

We circle the covert along its edge, then muck around in the center. It's nice in there, with plenty of dense but not-too-thorny shrubs, a mixture of gray dogwood, flowering dogwood, honeysuckle, barberry, and crabapples; several of the shrubs are festooned with bittersweet, the eye-catching gold-and-scarlet berries hanging on the vines. A good number of thornapples, and only a little of the detested multiflora rose. We hunt for quite a ways without making contact with game. Then Caillie starts working scent, and a woodcock gusts up on my left. It's a quick shot, and I drop the bird with the right barrel. When Caillie brings the woodcock in, I kneel to accept it. I pet my spaniel, telling her what a good dog she is. She wags her whole body while trying to lick my face. I draw the moment out. Every bird I bag is a beautiful, poignant thing. Every bird that my dog brings to my hand is a gift, a symbol of the communication and cooperation that flows between hunting partners of different species.

Woodcock are magical birds, the way they just show up in the coverts. They are as beautiful in their own subtle way as any warbler in its brilliant spring plumage. I like to see woodcock up close every so often, to confirm yet again that they're real. There is something keen and special in holding and hefting them; and there's something essential in my eating a meal or two of woodcock each fall. The only way I can do any of those things is to hunt woodcock and kill them.

I put the woodcock in my game pouch, nod to Carl, and we resume the hunt. Finally, without having moved any more birds, we're back at the turnaround. We case the guns and get into the truck. Unfortunately, today is a work day for me: This afternoon I have scheduled an interview with a scientist for an article I am writing about her research, and now I must head home, get myself cleaned up, and drive in to the university. Back at the house, Carl and I eat lunch, and I leave him ensconced in an easy chair, browsing through a book about (what else?) English shotguns. He plans to take a nap, then head out to try to fill his three-bird woodcock limit. If he's successful, and if there is still time left in the day, he says he'll hit the Jay Place for grouse.

~

When I get home in the evening, I find out that Carl's nap lasted somewhat longer than he'd anticipated, leaving him just enough time to drive to Port Matilda and hunt the Ballfield Covert again. There, at day's end, he flushed and killed his third woodcock.

As the evening stretches on, my thoughts are not about the interview I conducted, fascinating though it was (the scientist showed me waterlogged pieces of what is likely the pirate Blackbeard's flagship, whose identity she is helping to confirm by determining the species of the wood recovered from a wreck off the North Carolina coast). Nor do I want to dwell on the morning's woodcock hunt, or the inherent beauty and utility of English shotguns, or where we ought to go tomorrow, although in fact the conversation touches on all of those subjects. Rather, I find myself wanting to reminisce with Carl about hunts we have made together in the past.

We both remember the first time we shared a covert. Carl had come up to Centre County in the company of a mutual friend, a fellow with whom I had worked at the Pennsylvania Game Commission. As best as we can reconstruct it, the hunt took place in 1975. I took Carl and Lew to what was, at that time, my best covert: a brushy farm on Bald Eagle Mountain, above the village of Julian, where the road, unpaved back then, makes a hairpin turn. The covert commenced at the hairpin and extended away from the road to the east; it was good for woodcock and grouse. Although the hunt took place more than a quarter of a century ago, both Carl and I remember it. We had no dog. We went tramping in a line through the brush. I was on the uphill end, Lew was in the middle, and Carl anchored the bottom. A grouse got up, between and slightly behind Lew and me. The grouse flashed downhill, and I yelled "Bird!" and Carl turned and tumbled it. Back then he was using a Beretta over-and-under, a 20 gauge that he still owns and that has accounted for a truckload of game.

That shot impressed me. I have been impressed by Carl's skill with a shotgun many times since then. However, I am more impressed by his respect for the gamebirds, which has never dwindled. I am impressed, as well, by his respect for the land that supports grouse and woodcock and pheasants, as well as the other wild creatures. And by his respect for the tradition of hunting, particularly as it is exemplified by the relationship that has grown up between us.

Carl lives in Lebanon County, in southeastern Pennsylvania. There, winding creeks divide the fertile landscape into gentle and irregular hills that resemble the swell of a great sea. The limestone soil is farmed intensively. The human population in the region has risen steadily over the last decades. In years past, early in the fall I would travel down to Carl's to hunt mourning doves. Doves are among the most challenging of wingshooting targets, and on the times when we hunted them together, we generally had plenty of action. But nothing came close to the day we found the wheatfield. I should say The Wheatfield: the day and the place remain so prominent in my memory that I think of them now in the upper case.

The mourning dove, *Zenaida macroura*, is one species of gamebird that has not dwindled during recent decades. Far from it: the population has burgeoned in many parts of North America. Mourning doves thrive in farmland, where they feed on seeds, anything from weed seeds the size of a pinhead to wheat grains and kernels of corn left in the fields after the harvest. But the real reason doves have become so plentiful is that they can live in the suburbs that are obliterating the habitats of many other species. Among houses and lawns, doves find ample food, plus a nice mix of trees and shrubs for nesting. Doves are semicolonial nesters: a single tree may support as many as ten nests. The nests are shoddily built, and frequently one can see the pair of small white eggs by looking up through the flimsy structure of twigs and sticks upon which they were laid. A pair of doves may raise two or three broods in a summer.

Zipping along through the ether, doves make for challenging wing-shooting. When a dove spots a hunter crouching in the corn, it may flare suddenly and juke and change directions and go tearing off. I'm not a very good dove shot, unless I can do my work close in: the long chances and the necessity for leading the target often defeat me. When I spot doves heading my way, I avert my pale face, count slowly to myself (one thousand one, one thousand two, one thousand three), then pop up and go to work at a distance of twenty yards. Sometimes I get my share of the birds, and I have even bagged my limit of twelve when hunting with Carl. The quick-and-easy technique applies to field-dressing a dove: you basically rip the bird apart using your hands, and extract the breast, which is dark and dense, a succulent nugget of meat. Dove breasts are wonderful fare, especially when grilled over charcoal: I can polish off a half-dozen or more at a sitting.

Mourning doves are not very plentiful in Centre County, so I don't often hunt them here. But there are millions of doves—literally millions, by the time the summer breeding has ended—in southeastern Pennsylvania. On the afternoon that we ended up at The Wheatfield, the dove hunting had started out slowly. Carl, Jerry, and I had sat tucked back into the first row of corn adjacent to some newly mown alfalfa. Doves flew over us in good numbers, but even though we had set out decoys and carefully remained hidden among the tall green stalks, the sleek gray birds wouldn't give our field a second glance. Carl left for a time, and when he returned he announced that he'd found "the mother lode": a field where the wheat crop had failed and the farmer had mowed down the grain and left it. When we arrived there, it reminded me of a scene from the Alfred Hitchcock film *The Birds.* No sound and very little motion came from the massed doves occupying the field; only a slight shuffling of gray bodies and, in the foreground, the raising of hundreds of heads.

The field was covered with doves. Jerry, a wildlife biologist experienced at aerial waterfowl surveys, scanned the terrain, figured for a while, and hazarded the guess that at least two thousand doves were feeding in the stubble, with almost that many in a plowed field next to the wheat.

The dogs—my Jenny, and Carl's Labrador, Seneca—yelped as they caught sight of the incomers streaming into the field and landing in front of us. We got out of the car and began dumping cartridges into our vests, fumbling and dropping the hulls, because who could take his eyes off the doves? We split up and marched off along the edges of the field. I saw a formation of five come winging toward Carl. When he shot, it seemed that the whole field lifted into the air. I found a low spot choked with weeds—foxtails, smartweed, dock—and stamped down a place to kneel. Jenny was almost frantic, there were so many birds in the air; at first I had to leash her and put my foot on the leash's free end. Over the next hour, I shot at many doves. The empty shells mounded up on the ground in front of me. So did the doves retrieved by my spaniel. The doves' feet were pink, their breasts were pale lavender, and their bellies were salmon; little azure rings stood out like spectacles around their eyes

There were so many doves in that field, and so many other doves wanting to get into the field, that it didn't seem they paid us any attention. Our hunt was over too soon. The limit of a dozen seemed a ridiculous figure considering the superabundance of doves—still they came pouring into the field, picking up the waste grain—and yet the number also seemed more than enough.

When there were still good numbers of wild pheasants in southeastern Pennsylvania, and enough open land so that hunting them remained possible, I enjoyed spending a couple of days at Carl's in November. I remember Jenny's first ringneck: she didn't flush the rooster, but she retrieved it. Neither she nor Seneca had told us a bird was present. We were working the weedy edges of a small limestone quarry when the cockbird flushed. It got up nearer to Carl, but as it fought for height, it curled toward me. On the edge of my vision I watched Carl start to mount his shotgun, then lower it. It is a secure feeling, knowing that your partner will not chance a shot in your direction. As far as I can tell, greed for game has never motivated Carl; I wish I could say the same for myself. On this occasion, I was happy to swing my shotgun's muzzles through the pheasant's long golden tail, swing ahead through the body, through the glittering white neck ring and the carmine cheek patch ("Shoot 'em in the bill" was my mentor, Bob Bell's, terse advice), and touch the trigger. The bird fell in a patch of sunlit foxtails, and Jenny grabbed him. I have a photo of Jenny, looking like a gangly adolescent, sitting with me and the pheasant in front of Carl's woodpile.

After a while, we didn't hunt pheasants in Lebanon County. There were too many new houses, and most of the weedy fields had been put into production, the fencerows bulldozed into oblivion so that huge tractors could work in long straight lines; and, except on public land, of which there was relatively little, the pheasants were about gone.

However, we were building a separate tradition: Carl's visits to Bald Eagle Valley became a high point for our hunting each year, a total immersion in the thing we liked doing best. At first, Carl came up for a couple of days, and later it became a full week. We settled on the first week in November: the first week of general small game season, and usually the best week for the woodcock flights.

I pour Carl another two fingers of Scotch, then freshen my own glass.

Do you remember when we hunted at the Cemetery, and you flushed that grouse at the top of the slope, and it came barreling down toward me, and I swung and hit it hard, and the bird was going so fast that it sailed way, way downhill, and it took a hundred paces before I got to where it fell?

Do you remember when we found that covert south of the county line, the one we called the Sleeping Gent? How we looked in through the glass pane in the farmhouse door, and there's this old man asleep in a chair, and we talked it over and then went ahead and rapped on the door long and hard enough to wake him? And how he wasn't a bit grumpy, and said sure, go ahead and hunt. I know we flushed birds that day, but did we get any? When was the last time we tried that covert? Would it be worth it, heading down that way tomorrow?

Do you remember that time at Ted's Place, when that huge thick-necked buck went slinking out in front of us? Looked like he was walking on his knees, he was so low to the ground, and he crossed right next to you, and I don't think he even knew you were there.

Do you remember the time in Pufferbelly, when you were working Jenny down by the creek, I think you'd just killed a grouse, and I was up closer to the tracks, maybe a hundred yards away from you, and I scared that turkey gobbler out of the top of a pine tree? The season had just opened on them, and I was carrying the Harrison & Hussey 16, and I swung for his head and fired the choke barrel. I can still see the way he came down, like a helicopter with one of its blades missing. We had a heck of a time maneuvering to get the final shot in.

Do you remember the day you killed a grouse, a pheasant, and a woodcock with the Moore & Grey? It was the first time you used a hammergun in the field, and I gave you all kinds of grief, said you'd be lucky if you even got a shot off.

Do you remember the time Jenny slit her ear on a thornbush and hunted for the rest of the day covered with blood? Every time it stopped bleeding, she'd shake her head and open the cut up again. You were worried about her losing so much blood, but it didn't seem to slow her down. She flushed and fetched a couple of pheasants for us.

Do you remember the time we flushed I bet it was twenty woodcock in that one little patch down at Sayers, and it was the first time Caillie had ever really gotten into a flight? She didn't believe there were that many woodcock in the world. In fact, it may have been the first time she ever encountered a woodcock. I was trying to steady her that fall. That whole idea went out the window then and there.

Do you remember?

How could you forget?

Chapter 13

Carl and I have developed this method of communicating in the field: I yell his name, and he stops in his tracks, then hitches up his hearing protectors on the ear closest to me. We say what we need to say (usually how we should work a given patch of cover), he puts his earmuffs back on, and we proceed.

It can be tough, trying to hunt while wearing muffs. I know, because I've tried it.

About ten years ago both Carl and I decided we could not afford to lose any more of our hearing to shotgun blasts. I'm not sure how much hearing Carl has lost, but I know I've squandered far too much of this precious sense. I remember the moment I knew I had to do something about it. I was looking at a yellowthroat perched in a shrub. The bird—a male, with a bright yellow throat and belly, set off by a black face mask—lifted his head and opened his bill. I listened, expecting to hear the familiar *wichity, wichity, wichity* song. But all I heard was the high tone—not quite a ringing or a buzzing, but something in between—that is a near-constant presence in my head.

I knew I had damaged my hearing in the past. When I was a boy, I used to shoot .22-caliber rifles in an indoor range. Ten of us would lie on mats, side by side, firing at paper targets fifty feet away; when I came out of the gallery my ears would ring for hours. As a teenager I mowed lawns for pocket money, pushing a loud mower. Building my house, I used an array of power tools and pounded in thousands of nails. I have heated my home with firewood for three decades, and for the first several years I did not wear hearing protection when running my chainsaw.

All of those noises, and many others, harm one's hearing: they trample down the cilia, tiny hairlike structures in the inner ear that pick up the vibrations that are the physical basis of sound. Humans evolved to have sharp hearing, the better to detect predators and prey. Our ears are not designed to withstand loud machine-generated noises. A few years back, I got together with my old college roommate, who grew up on a farm and drove a tractor for hours on end; although not yet fifty years old, he wore a hearing aid in each ear. I learned of a man living near me who had been a lathe operator. He keeps a radio turned on low in his bedroom all night long: without that white noise in the background, the ringing in his ears won't let him sleep. Hearing loss, I read, is a cumulative process. The more harmful noises you are exposed to, the more your hearing erodes, and the louder and more insistent the buzzing and ringing become. The condition is called tinnitus.

I realized I was missing many sounds in nature, mainly in the higher frequencies: subtle rustlings in the leaves (I'm a lot less effective as a deer hunter nowadays); the intricate layers of sound emanating from wind in the trees or a tumbling stream; and many bird calls, such as the whistle of a hawk or the soft notes of a flycatcher. I had trouble following conversations in places where there was background noise, such as a crowded restaurant or when riding in a car.

I would go hunting, take half a dozen shots, and my ears would ring for the rest of the day. I tried wearing ear muffs when afield but found I couldn't pick up the beating of a grouse's wings or the twittering flight of a woodcock: I'd see a gamebird out of the corner of my eye and realize I would have had a shot at it, if only I'd heard the bird taking off. I actually considered quitting hunting, because I wanted to do it at a reasonable level of competence and did not wish to sacrifice what was left of my hearing. When

Will failed to show an interest in hunting, I was disappointed but also to a certain extent relieved: my son would not damage his hearing through shooting (though he's doing his part by listening to loud music nowadays).

Fortunately, technology helped me out. I bought, at no little expense, a pair of electronic hearing protectors made by a high-tech company in Oregon. They are powered by tiny batteries, and they fit in my ears like hearing aids. I turn a small wheel on each, to amplify the sound of my surroundings: with a little practice, I found I could pretty much reproduce the natural sound environment. When those ingenious devices pick up a gunshot or some other loud, impulsive sound, a circuit immediately shuts off, barring the pulse of energy from entering my ears and further damaging the cilia. The electronics aren't perfect: when conditions are dry, the protectors amplify my footfalls so that it sounds like I'm trampling on cornflakes. The hearing protectors have shown me that I've been damaging my hearing in unexpected ways. Not only do they cut out when I fire a shot, but they shut down when I blow on my dog whistle. I wear the protectors when training dogs, hunting deer, and working on building projects. They won't restore any of the hearing I've lost, but they will prevent damage in the future.

For many years Carl and I participated in a study designed to monitor grouse and woodcock populations in Pennsylvania. The concept was that bird hunters should keep track of all the grouse and woodcock they flushed, noting the numbers down on a paper card at the end of each day afield. At the season's end, survey participants entered the numbers onto a form and mailed it to a game commission biologist. The biologist used the raw data in an effort to spot trends: the ups and downs of gamebird populations, the timing of the peak woodcock migration.

A problem with hunting while wearing any kind of ear protection—including my electronic plugs—is that one misses a certain percentage of the flushes: they happen a bit too far away, or when one is setting foot on crunchy leaves or twigs. A few years ago, I decided to stop counting flushes. I did not want to send in flawed data that might skew the study's results. Also, for me the act of counting had begun to get in the way of fully enjoying a day in the coverts. Keeping track of flushes distracted me from an activity that I wished to keep as pure and simple as possible. In hunting, one needs to absorb and process many factors: The position and movement of the dog. The wind direction. (Depending on the lay of the land, I will try to hunt into the wind, so the dog can use her nose to the best effect.) The specific route I should pick through a given patch of cover, to afford the greatest number of shooting opportunities, while not impaling myself on thorns or getting tripped by vines or having my hat snatched off by low branches. More important, I wanted to concentrate on the sounds, sights, and sensations that the natural world has to offer.

Carl and I have progressed from using pump-action shotguns to light, maneuverable side-by-sides. We have quit counting our flushes, the better to soak up the experience of bird hunting. As hunters, we've changed in other ways, as well: now in our fifties, we get tired more quickly than we used to. We try to keep fit—Carl plays volleyball, and I jog—but the joints are wearing down, and the stamina isn't what it used to be. Nor are we so keen to fill our game pouches every time out. Where once we hunted from dawn to dusk, now we're apt to get into the coverts a bit later in the morning. Rarely do we keep at it until the light has begun to fail, despite the fact that the last hour of the day is often the most productive hour of grouse hunting, when the birds have left the spots where they've been hiding—the boughs of conifers, the tangled hearts of thorn patches—and ventured forth to fill their crops before dark.

I hope that my more relaxed attitude toward bagging birds is counter-balanced by the fact that I am now a better wingshot than when I first started hunting. In general, I think I make better use of the chances that come my way. I have shot at enough grouse over the years so that now I don't get as rattled when one flushes: excited, yes; panicked, not usually. I know enough to look hard at a bird, separate it from its environment, figure out where its flight path will take it, and, using a minimum of effort, to direct my shotgun to intercept that path. I don't rush my shots—at least not as frequently as I once did. My more-laid-back disposition also stems from a waning of the specific desire to kill birds. I don't need to justify my

A HUNTER'S BOOK OF DAYS
130

time afield by the numbers of grouse and woodcock brought to bag. Often it feels better to let a flushed bird go, rather than to follow it up, flushing it again and again until I get a shot.

When I'm shooting well, there's not much of an intellectual process taking place. It's more a matter of concentrating on the bird and letting muscle memory and reflexes do the rest. If someone asked me how I made a certain shot on a grouse, I might be hard-pressed to put it into words. Often I don't consciously think about raising the gun or pushing the safety off. I don't generally consider which trigger to pull, the front one (for close-in shots, which are the majority of chances offered) or the rear one (for the occasional bird that gets up beyond twenty or so yards).

The bird launches itself into the air, my attention is riveted on it, the shotgun's butt finds the familiar pocket in my shoulder, and the shot reaches out like a deadly finger pointing at its mark.

When I'm shooting well.

However, I'm not shooting well now, in what may be my last bird season in Pennsylvania.

~

Thursday dawns clear, with a pink-tinted sky and a breeze stirring in the north. We start off by driving thirty miles, picking our way through rush-hour traffic around State College and Penn State; we plan to explore a covert on the eastern side of the county, where a game commission forester told Carl he'd seen "a lot of grouse" earlier in the year. The area is part of a tract that the commission is considering buying and turning into a new state game land.

I have spent a lot of time hiking in the wilder parts of Centre County. I haven't been to this place in years, but I know just where Carl means when he describes it. In that forested mountain valley, a friend and I once camped out on a cold winter night. We were yanked out of sleep when a barred owl opened up, at full volume, from the hemlock under which we'd pitched our tent: the call, *hoohoo-hoohoo . . . hoo-hoo-hoohooaw* (usually described as "Who cooks for you, who cooks for you-all?") made the hair stand up on my neck. I brought Nancy to this same valley on a day in early spring; it was one of our first dates. We hiked along on a faint trail, until we came to a log. Lifting my foot to step across, I heard a sound that signaled pure, unadulterated menace: like an electric wire sparking on the ground, or a chunk of fat thrown into a red-hot skillet. Before my mind even registered "Snake!" my body had thrown itself backward. I peered over the log at a timber rattler coiled where I had almost set my foot. The snake buzzed again, its rattle blurring. I was impressed by the power and danger that emanated from the snake. I was even more impressed when the woman who would eventually become my wife did not scream or urge me to kill the snake but evinced a keen interest in the handsome, banded, charcoal-gray serpent.

Carl and I park next to a gated road. I'm amazed at how this place has changed since the last time I was here. It has been logged, and logged hard, probably to salvage timber following the gypsy moth invasion that swept through the county in the 1980s. Where once stood mature red, white, and chestnut oaks, now lie decomposing logging debris and fallen trees bare of their bark, strewn about like old bleached bones. Above all of this clutter stand unthrifty looking red maples and a host of black birch saplings. With the leaves fallen off the maples and birches, one can see for hundreds of yards through the woods. It's apparent that the oaks—either killed by the feeding of gypsy-moth caterpillars, or their stump sprouts browsed long and hard by too many deer—will not be replenishing the forest here. I wonder what will happen to the ecosystem, following the loss of an entire group of sylvan species that once supported a food chain reaching from acorn-eating chipmunks to chipmunk-eating rattlesnakes. This does not look like a healthy woodland to me. Other forces may be at work here, as well: Some ecologists speculate that acid rain, sent to Pennsylvania by coal-burning power plants in the Midwest, is leaching away nutrients from the soil—soil that is very thin, in this rocky upland setting—so that it will no longer support the growth of some trees, perhaps including the oaks. In many places, hay-scented fern, an acid-tolerant plant, grows so thickly that tree seedlings can't get a start.

It doesn't take long for Carl and me to conclude that, despite what the forester saw, or thinks he saw, grouse are not plentiful in this place. We hunt for several hundred yards, with Caillie combing through the mountain laurel understory, and she doesn't show any sign of picking up bird scent. I'm not surprised. "A lot of grouse" can mean one thing to a person who doesn't actually hunt grouse, and another thing to someone who assiduously pursues *Bonasa umbellus.* To the former, a late-summer brood, with birds flushing and arrowing off in all directions, looks like a super-abundance of game. A seasoned grouse hunter wouldn't get too excited at finding a single brood in this sort of borderline-to-impoverished habitat; he might check back later in the year, but he wouldn't harbor hopes of moving many birds.

We're not all that far from the public hunting area in the Bald Eagle Valley, and we quickly decide to head there. We drive through two notches in the mountain ridges. En route, we decide to try a large cover stretching south and east of the town of Howard, on the south shore of the lake created by the damming of Bald Eagle Creek. I haven't hunted the area yet this year; in the past, it has been a good place for woodcock when the flight birds are in, and I have taken the occasional grouse there. Once again, the place where we park is littered with beer bottles and cans and assorted other trash. All too many ne'er-do-wells live in the valley; in the past, while hunting or training dogs on the public area, I've come across hidden marijuana plantings, as well as clandestine partying spots like this one. I'm glad I usually have a shotgun with me when I come here.

The Howard covert is a mix of mature woods and old boggy fields grown up with willow shrubs, blackberries, thornapples, crabapples, and multiflora rose. Walking side by side, Carl and I hunt for almost a mile through apparently excellent cover without raising a woodcock or a grouse. Then Caillie picks up some scent. A wind is quartering in off the lake from the right. Caillie grabs a scrap of scent here, another scrap there, and it doesn't take long before I'm sure we are following a running pheasant. We hunt along in this manner for a hundred yards. Then another hundred. Carl is off on the left, checking out some likely looking woodcock cover. I decided to outwit the pheasant: I hup Caillie, then loop out on the left and stride ahead quickly for about sixty yards. Once in place, I give two toots on the whistle to release Caillie. She picks up the trail and follows it toward me, and right away she flushes the pheasant. It's a hen. But the bird outwits me. It curls up and back over the dog, denying me a shot. It flies back the way we have come, curving around and following the lake edge, until it's out of sight.

I whistle Caillie in. I think about following the bird, but clearly Carl would rather hunt onward.

We trek a long way, rooting through the thick cover and walking through the stands of open woods that separate the old fields. We flush no more upland birds, although we do raise some ducks: a drake mallard and three blacks. They come rocketing up out of a gut where the lake extends back inland at the mouth of a small stream. Light-catching drops of water fall from their bellies as they bank and head for the center of the lake. Quite wary, they took to the air before we got within gun range, although in any case we're not hunting waterfowl and don't have the requisite steel-shot shells needed to legally take ducks.

Another quarter-mile of blank cover, and we find ourselves in an absolute hell of multiflora rose and tartarian honeysuckle—nonnative plants both, introduced long ago to improve game habitat and now choking out the native vegetation. As thick as the cover is, it doesn't seem to hold any birds, or else they are adept at getting out of our way. Finally we extract ourselves from the vegetation and hike back toward the truck along the railroad tracks.

After lunch, it's back to the Endless Circle. Quickly we are into woodcock again. I handle Caillie in front of me, while Carl works slightly to one side: off there, he may get shooting at a bird the dog flushes, and he can also explore adjacent patches of cover and perhaps put up a bird himself. The first woodcock flutters up in front of him. It's a hen, and the bird twists away between the trees; Carl kills it. Then Caillie flushes another woodcock. I miss it with a snapshot, and as the bird crosses in front of Carl, he drops it.

Farther on, I pull Caillie in using the whistle. She angles toward me,

A HUNTER'S BOOK OF DAYS

134

then crouches for an instant on her back legs, springs into a clump of shrubs, and puts up a woodcock. As the bird rises, it does something I've never seen a timberdoodle do before: it collides with a blackberry cane about two feet off the ground, falls back down, nearly gets nabbed by the dog, flushes again, and flies off again in a different direction. I have a clear shot, and I take this luckless bird as it slips between a hardwood and a pine. Caillie finds the dead woodcock in a dogwood thicket and brings it to me. I stroke the sleek white fur on her chin while praising her. The woodcock is a smallish one, clearly a male and probably a bird of the year. I wonder where he hatched, what boggy fields and old farms he has supped in and slept in during his trek southward, which has now come to an end.

We swing around to the north in the orb-shaped covert. We flush two more woodcock but don't get shooting at them. Finally, after we have hunted most of the way back to the turnaround, Carl puts up another woodcock and takes it cleanly; it is his third bird gotten within the hour, giving him his limit.

It is now the middle of the afternoon, and we must decide where to go next. A grouse covert on the way home? We could try Burnt Baker or the Jay Place, but both are steep and rugged, and we're tired after all the marching we've already done. We decide to hunt elsewhere on the relatively flat ground of the public shooting area, where there's a chance of finding pheasants. We drive down the valley to the same general area where I bagged two woodcock and Carl got a pair of pheasants on Monday. We park along the highway, which hums with traffic. We walk down into a cut hayfield, then along an old fencerow leading to a section of aspens. We turn east and enter a broad strip of cover next to the lake.

We haven't gone far before Caillie's tail tells us there are birds in here. An instant later five pheasants come busting out of a head-high thicket, four drab hens and a red-cheeked rooster cackling madly. I remember writing something to the effect that flushing birds don't panic me as much as they did when I was a beginning hunter. I would have to describe as a symptom of "panic" the way I start to shoot at the rooster, then switch off to take a hen, then change my mind and settle, more or less, on a second, somewhat closer hen. As a result, I don't cheek the stock properly, and for the second time today I miss a bird that then flies past Carl's unerring gun. The hen collapses in a puff of tan feathers. In Britain, hunters describe this sequence of events as "having your eye wiped." It does nothing to improve a shooter's confidence. I whistle and yell at Caillie until she hups. Carl walks over and picks up the hen.

"Good shot," I tell him, probably more gruffly than I mean to. I stand there for a while, working on getting my anger and frustration under control. We're having fun here. The sky is a sweet and untroubled blue, and the low sun is painting the aspens with a golden light. Tall blades of grass hiss and tick in the wind. A lone mallard drake flies high overhead, his wings taking swift economical beats, his gray belly catching the warm light; the duck's head, a knout at the end of the long slender neck, switches from side to side as the fowl observes us.

We decide to follow three of the pheasants, which flew down into a thick area near the lake. Carl takes the uphill side, while I slog along through mud and rank grass, using the whistle to keep the spaniel in tight. Caillie is as birdy as she can be. I try to make her cover the ground thoroughly and not overrun any of the brushy patches where birds may be hiding. The excitement keeps building the farther into the cover we get. Yes, these are stocked pheasants. No, they are no more native than the multiflora rose and tartarian honeysuckle I was bemoaning earlier in the day. But the birds are wild and fast-flying, they challenge our shooting skills, they test the dog, and they have been put down in a handsome stretch of land.

Caillie starts working scent between Carl and me. Suddenly a hen is up, barreling between the saplings, left to right, heading toward the lake. It's my bird, and I turn to face the water and wait until the hen clears the cover. The pheasant is aimed for the other side of the lake, an overgrown hillside about three hundred yards distant. I swing ahead of the hen and pull the trigger. The gun thumps me on the shoulder, and I can see the white shot cup arcing out past the hen, even as the pattern crashes home. The pheasant's wings collapse, and the bird is driven sideways. It splashes down in the water.

"Caillie!" She enters the lake and swims out the forty or so yards to where the pheasant's momentum has taken it. Caillie snatches the floating bird, pivots, and paddles back.

We hunt ahead another twenty yards, and the rooster flushes. He is flecked all over with bronze, green, and black. Crowing, he reaches for the treetops. I miss him with the right barrel and kill him with the left. He goes down heavily. Caillie heads in for the retrieve. As she picks up the pheasant, I notice Carl opening his gun and extracting a fired cartridge. I know that Carl doesn't often miss. I have demonstrated, repeatedly, that I do miss. An odd situation, this. I can tell that Carl knows he has killed the rooster. I am equally sure that I corrected my first miss and centered the bird with the choke barrel.

The weight of evidence is not on my side. It seems a reasonable, if difficult, thing to do, to hand my friend the bird and let him pouch it. By abdicating my claim on the pheasant I allow that my eye has been wiped thrice.

We work toward the next break in the cover, a grassy road, where we expect a bird may hold and flush, if it has run on ahead. At this point Carl isn't really hunting, having taken his limit of both woodcock and pheasants; he's carrying his gun loaded and ready in case a grouse gets up, but that's not very likely. I push through to the edge of the brush and wait while Caillie beats through the cover, but nothing comes of it.

We turn and hunt back toward where the truck is parked. On my right, the sun is sinking. The white coat of the dog flickers behind the goldenrod stems. The gun feels good in my hands. I'm pleasantly tired. I am satisfied with this day, even though I haven't seen a grouse, even though my shooting has been all too shoddy. Despite the thorns that pluck at my brush pants and nick home every now and then, it feels like I'm floating through the cover.

"Woodcock!"

Carl flushed it. The bird flies straight at me. Its head looks like a small brown-and-black ball. The bill is long and slightly opened. The woodcock pumps its wings and flares its stubby tail as it comes to earth gently, about five feet from my boots. I look down on it. The woodcock gives a little shrug of its wings, and seems to gather in on itself. I stand there, and it's just me and the woodcock in the covert. I glance away, and when I look back it takes a second for my eyes to pick up the bird again. The woodcock looks like a bunch of leaves molded together, then dropped on the ground. The bird's dark ingenuous eyes are examining me, too. I wonder what it sees.

I can hear Carl moving ahead through the brush. I suppose I should account for my spaniel, who is ranging off to the right, probably a bit too far out by now. I watch the woodcock, and it doesn't move a muscle. It squats there, its camouflage blending it into its own world, a world I can scarcely enter. Taking quiet, slow steps, I move away.

In the strange, equivocal way of a hunter, it is not then disagreeable to me when my spaniel drives another woodcock up out of the brush, and the bird is flying fast, and I swing my gun and take it. Caillie fetches. My shot has broken one of the woodcock's wings and stove in its bill; blood seeps from between the bird's mandibles. The eyes, vacant of life, are dark and quiet pools. I put the woodcock in my game pouch. I release the spaniel, and hunt onward.

We reach the far edge of the covert, up against the hayfield where we started working this section a couple of hours ago. There's a bulge of land next to the lake that I don't believe we covered on our initial sweep. I direct Caillie into the area, a dense stand of goldenrod, hawthorn, and multiflora rose, with a few bare-branched aspens. I am pleased with Caillie's work today, and with how well she has held up this week; she must be about played out, having hunted hard for four days straight. She's leaner than she was on Monday, despite the fact that I've doubled her rations. But she isn't flagging. She's hunting hard, and she's hunting for the gun.

She casts out and works back into the wind, which is lessening now that the sun is going down. We make a slow circle through the cover, exploring it all the way to the water's edge.

On our way back up the slope, Caillie drives a bird out of the grass. It comes up between me and the sun. I can't tell what it is, although it is bigger than a woodcock and so almost certainly a pheasant: it does not cackle, which means it's probably a hen. I can hear its wings beating. I get my feet sorted out. I check to be sure Carl is out of the line of fire, which he is. I lean toward the flush and look hard to distinguish the bird. All of this has happened in about a second, yet it seems like a remarkably long time. The bird passes in front of the sun. I swing through and ahead of the silhouetted form, and shoot. I strain to see if my shot has hit. There's a big cloud of sparkling, sunlit feathers, and Carl calls out in a tone full of satisfaction (and maybe relief): "Good shot!"

Caillie retrieves the hen pheasant. The cloud of feathers drifts down, expanding as it falls.

Chapter 14

〜

We're taking a breather high up in Burnt Baker. Carl is a few yards down the slope from me, below a mess of grapevines, blackberry canes, sumac, and maple brush; by leaning forward I can just make out a swatch of his orange vest. Caillie sits hupped next to me. Above us, small white clouds race across a deep blue sky. Wind shakes the trees, knocking down leaves. As they fall, the leaves slap against branches and the ground. Around us, the oak-clad hills and ridges shine a bright bronze, with hints of purple in the shady creases and gaps and beneath the swift-moving cloud shadows.

We're finding birds; not a bundle of them, but enough to keep us primed and ready.

On the way up the hollow, Caillie flushed a woodcock that offered a tough shot as it twisted up and then went slanting behind a pine. I fired, knowing I probably wouldn't hit the bird (I didn't) and understanding that the report would alert Carl to a gamebird on the wing. The woodcock flew downhill, and I saw Carl raise the Lancaster. The woodcock fell at the edge of an aspen stand. At Carl's shot, a grouse flushed on the far side of the same stand. I had a live cartridge in the choke barrel, but didn't shoot at the grouse because it was too far out. I whistled Caillie in, and we picked our way downhill to help Carl find his woodcock.

When I handed the bird to my friend, he looked at the woodcock—a hen—with a puzzled smile on his face. "I thought I was shooting at a grouse." He hefted the bird, then folded its wings shut in his hand. He put the woodcock in his game pouch. "It was just a brown blur flying through the brush."

"When you shot," I said, "a grouse got up between us. It flew up the hollow. It's somewhere out ahead."

"Let's see if we can raise it again."

"They're flushing wild."

Carl nodded. "It's the wind."

A wind making noise in the coverts—whining through the branches, making the trees creak, rustling the leaves—puts grouse on edge. It deprives them of their hearing, which, along with their vision, is an important sense for detecting and evading predators. When it's windy, grouse apparently decide that the odds of their surviving are better if they flush—even though flight exposes them to aerial predators like hawks—than if they wait around to see what it is that's stalking across the land.

Carl would very much like to bag a grouse, and I, too, would be glad to see him get one. During his two most recent visits to Centre County, our only real action has been on woodcock and pheasants. In five days of hunting in 2001 and four days in 2000, he failed to kill a grouse. In 2000, when conditions were so dry, we ended up hunting mainly in low-lying areas, and he didn't even get a shot at a grouse. Nor did he take a grouse during the several other hunts he made in coverts closer to his home over the last two years. He told me he'd gotten "no more than two to four shots each season, none of which I'd call good opportunities."

Again it strikes me, how impoverished our gunning has been. We've been making do. Woodcock are exciting to hunt, but there is something about them—their naivete, I suspect—that keeps me from wanting to gun them too assiduously. Put-and-take pheasants, even when they require hard hunting and exacting wingshooting, don't compel me to be out there pounding the coverts day after day. But grouse are different. They are found in the best wild places. They are warier, and, in their difficult haunts, they challenge the gunner much more than do woodcock or pheasants. I have a special affection for grouse because they are native birds that live here year-round, taking whatever the weather dishes out, surviving even through times as tough as these last seven years have been.

I peer ahead through the dense cover on the steep slope. "Ready?" I call down to Carl. Caillie conveniently interprets this vocalization as a release command and starts to move out: I growl at her, making her stop, then take her by the collar and return her to where I'd placed her on hup. The master must be ever vigilant.

Carl has by now started forward, feeling his way past a shoal of greenbrier. I tell the spaniel: "Heel."

In 1994 I went hunting for red grouse in the high, rolling Grampian Mountains of central Scotland. I was one of five shooters, and, although I practiced long and hard before the trip, I was far and away the least experienced shot in our group. Where I had an advantage, however, was in my level of conditioning. We would climb a steep hill or clear a rise, and while the others in the line were huffing and puffing, staring at their boot tops, I was swinging on grouse that had spotted us and come whirring out of the heather. Often I ended up taking birds that were five or even ten yards closer to me than the ones my companions were gunning—a situation that actually let me hold my own in that group of topflight sporting clays competitors. I was fit because I jogged, and because I was used to hunting in places like Burnt Baker.

At Burnt Baker, small flat sandstone rocks by the thousands lie ready to grate and chatter under your boots. Fallen leaves hide damp sticks, the sticks with their long lengths pointing downhill, the better to slick your leg out from under you. Greenbrier and multiflora rose grab you by the elbow like determined city panhandlers. Fallen logs must be clambered over or detoured around. Slanting, hung-up trees and arrays of moldering branches left after logging force you to backtrack and twist and bend and sometimes to go crawling on your hands and knees. Grapevines wait to snare an arm, a hip, the pocket or armhole of your vest. Just try to shoot at a fast, evasive bird while picking your way through a series of such obstructions. Burnt Baker gives away nothing to the worst of the heather-clad slopes we climbed on that Highlands estate, including the one the gamekeeper and the dog handler referred to, with burred tongues and grins on their faces, as the Wall of Death. The Wall of Pretty Decent Footing and Open Shooting, was how I thought of it.

I'm brought out of this reverie by wingbeats. "Bird!" I call out, even as I realize that the grouse has flushed well in front of me and nowhere near Carl. It is the fourth grouse that has gone out unseen or having given us only a glimpse. In Burnt Baker, when a grouse takes flight at thirty yards, usually the best you can hope for is a closer reflush. I sometimes think I'd be better off hunting this covert with a pointing dog, a swift one that might get out in front, pinning the birds between two dangers. But on a dry, windy day such as this one, with the scenting conditions marginal and the grouse on edge, any dog would have a tough time of it. Today I'm essentially using Caillie as a nonslip retriever, making her walk along beside me (making her walk more or less close to me: it's a rare spaniel that will heel contentedly like a golden or a Lab), ready to be dispatched into particularly thick places and to recover a bird if one of us should bring one down—the odds of which seem slim on this, the final day of Carl's week with me in the Bald Eagle Valley.

We struggle across the top of Burnt Baker. We spend an hour, maybe longer, in the thickest—and what is usually the most productive part—of the covert. A couple more birds take flight, but neither offers a shot. Did they angle down the slope, or did they fly up onto the plateau? We can't be sure, since neither of us saw exactly where they went. We decide against the plateau and instead move a little ways down the grade. We reverse our heading and make a return pass through a slightly more open but still thick and excellent-appearing grouse habitat. At one point, when Carl is hidden behind some brush, I hear him shoot. I wait a few seconds before asking: "Get the bird?"

"No."

Hunting onward, we advance in fits and starts: Carl goes first, then stops. Caillie and I move up next, then pause. We try to go as quietly as we can. The tactic is designed to catch birds napping, to keep them holding tight until we get close to them. On our third pass across Burnt Baker, we have both stopped, facing forward and unfortunately having ignored a small grape tangle that lies between us. It is a thick, dangling coil composed of several vines whose rooted bases lie sprawled below a leaning maple. It looks like any of the four dozen grape tangles that we have already passed.

I thought for a moment of climbing up and checking it, but I listened to the defeatist in me saying that a grouse wouldn't be in there, the tangle is too thin, and anyway my legs feel like lead. I don't know if Carl went through a similar thought process, or if he even noticed the tangle. I take a step forward, and a grouse thunders out of it. I whirl toward the bird, but the grouse is flying fast, headed back the way we came, already too far for a shot. I look at the broad chestnut tail, the crested head, and the way the bird's body yaws slightly as it dodges between tree trunks. The grouse is gone in a twinkling. With the cover so thick, it's hard to say where it went.

Caillie whines, Carl smiles, and I shake my head.

We turn and follow, hoping to flush the bird again—a grouse will usually hold more tightly on a reflush—but this one seems to have disappeared. As we hunt, we keep giving up elevation. In the flats below the bowl we kick through a greenbrier-choked stream bottom. We check the pines at the old field's edge. Unwilling to admit defeat, we reverse our heading, climb the hill again, and make another pass through the good dense cover just below the most precipitous pitch of the slope.

Nothing.

We've had a week of tough hunting, and Carl has a long drive ahead of him this afternoon. It's getting on toward the time when he ought to start for home.

We should call it quits and walk back to the truck along the old lane, but nobody wants to give up yet. So we hunt down the hollow, wending our way past the gutted house foundation, along the sidehill with its grapevines and greenbrier patches, its blackberry clusters and sumac stands, and finally through the damp stream bottom. We do not flush any more birds. Altogether, in about four hours we raised one woodcock (the one that Carl shot) and had eight or nine flushes on grouse, perhaps on six individual birds. It's nothing like the old days. But it's better than what we've known in the last years.

~

Come evening, I'm sitting in the living room with a book propped open on my lap, trying to stay awake. With Carl gone and the masculine chitchat at an end, Nancy has reclaimed her place on the couch. Will sits at the other end of the couch. All of us, as is our wont, are reading.

I close my book, lean back in the chair, and take stock.

After five days of hunting, I have raspberry-colored puncture marks up and down my arms; I look like an addict, although one whose attachment is to *Bonasa umbellus* rather than to some controlled substance. Additional purple marks stipple my legs, particularly the tops of my thighs. I've got a big plum-colored bruise on the outside of one leg and can't for the life of me figure out where I picked it up. The right side of my nose is scratched and swollen, thanks to a catclaw briar. A tip of a broken thornapple needle remains lodged in one shoulder (I got it at the public hunting area on Thursday; it ought to work itself out in a day or so). My legs feel like they're held to my hips with rusty hinges. I'm tired enough that I actually look forward to going to work next week and sitting at a desk.

I'm not very keen on collecting numbers and keeping tally, and peoples' figures on the numbers of birds they've flushed and taken—statistics that some seem happy to reel off at a moment's notice—pretty much leave me cold. But I've been keeping notes this season, since it may be my last in Pennsylvania. I get out my notebook and total the birds that Carl and I took this year in my coverts. Thanks largely to his skill with a shotgun (a shotgun with external hammers, at that), the two of us bagged twenty-four gamebirds. Carl killed eleven woodcock and four pheasants. He didn't miss a shot on a pheasant, and he was almost as true on the woodcock. He missed the sole grouse he shot at, which proves he's human, I guess.

The dog work was fair to middling—at times, it was pretty good. I reach out a stockinged toe, place it on the Sizzle's ribs, and gently rock the supine spaniel, who thuds her tail on the rug. My shooting? I probably shot as poorly as I ever have over a five-day stretch. That's what happens when you don't practice enough before the season begins. I'm trying to forget how many times Carl wiped my eye. The quality of my shooting does not deplete the satisfaction I've gotten from our week together. And I did manage to take five woodcock, a couple of pheasants, and, on that memorable and abundant Tuesday, a brace of grouse. The first grouse I shot, down in Pufferbelly, the one that came rocketing up out of the thorns little more than an arm's length away, I'll carry around in my head for a long time—maybe forever.

In the open stove, orange and blue flames wrap around a chunk of chestnut oak, crackling and sending smoke up the chimney. As far as I can tell, not a single oak tree grows on our farm in Vermont. Up there the forests are composed mainly of beech, birch, maple, and ash. Aspen grows there, too, and grouse absolutely dote on aspen buds. In Vermont's Northeast Kingdom, the locals call ruffed grouse "partridges." Most of the birds have a grayish plumage, a somber garb compared to the warm and ruddy browns worn by the grouse I have hunted for so many years in Pennsylvania.

I think about the challenge of finding new bird coverts in Vermont. I will have to learn where the woodcock dwell in their passage, and where the grouse are at home. I hope Carl will make the long drive north to hunt with me. After all these years, I look forward to a return to good hunting—to those intensely focused moments when time stops, and a bird is hurtling through nature, and my hunter's instincts rise and tell me: take it.

Chapter 15

It's strange, after working for myself all these years, to be answering to someone else's schedule. It's also different (and gratifying) to earn a regular, sizable paycheck. My week with Carl burned up all of the vacation I had accumulated during my brief tenure so far this year at Penn State. And thus for the first time in recent memory, like someone who works at a mill, like the man or woman who fixes cars or sells insurance or teaches school, I'm limited to hunting on weekends.

Through the rest of November I have exactly three Saturdays on which I can get out and tramp the hills for grouse (hunting is not permitted on Sundays in Pennsylvania). But because I haven't encountered all that many birds, for the first two of those days I find other things to do: I take a long ride on my gelding. I split a couple of cords of firewood and stack it under the shed.

Soon after Carl left, Nancy drove to Vermont. She stayed with a friend, Claire, an artist who has remodeled two farmhouses, one of which, she told us, was in far worse condition than the house we bought. Nancy met with carpenters and got them started on demolishing the parts of the house that we know we won't keep. When they pulled down the old paneling and the wallpaper-covered plaster, they exposed the post-and-beam frame that lay hidden beneath: seven-by-seven-inch squared spruce timbers, their joints still tight, the massive framing members bearing the marks of the broad ax used to shape them. Based on where the house is sited, Claire judges that it was built around 1840. Even though it will be more expensive than demolishing the house and building anew, we decide to remodel, to save as much of the dwelling's history and character as we can by working around the hand-hewn frame. Nancy and Claire discussed where to put the rooms, and Claire sketched out a floorplan and a redesign of the exterior—although we won't really know how much work will need to be done, and to what extent we may have to modify those plans, until the demolition gets farther along.

Will has been attending Bald Eagle Area High School for almost three months now. In some ways, it's a rough place, with a fair number of children from families split up by drinking and drugs. There's something of an anti-achievement and an anti-intellectual attitude in place: if you're too smart, you are looked down on, especially if you don't play a sport. Will is in the marching band, and has made friends with a lot of students. Nor is he having difficulty with the work. Just the opposite: it's too easy for him. During middle school, for three years leading up to this year, he attended a technology-oriented charter school, where he was pushed to learn as much as he could. Now, back in the public system, where the teachers sometimes seem to be babysitting the students rather than instructing and challenging them, he's often bored.

We're thinking more and more of that academy on the hill overlooking Lyndonville, Vermont—if we moved up there sooner, rather than later, Will could attend his final three years of high school at the Lyndon Institute. My job at Penn State is a temporary one, lasting through next June, when Nancy's yearlong leave of absence will end. The idea has been that she'll go back to the university, and I'll resume working on my own. But her ultimate goal is to be a freelance writer as well. She's tired of the corporate world of a big university, and she's tired of her job. After having done it myself for a couple of months now, I can understand why she doesn't like the commute: what was once a pleasant drive in the country is now a gauntlet of construction barricades and flagmen and stoplights that must be run along with the thousands of other drivers heading to the university and to the businesses and stores in and around State College.

We're coming closer to a decision—one that perhaps we made back in June, when we stood on that grassy hill in the gentle rain, listening to hermit thrushes calling from the green woods. A decision that we may have arrived at while hiking on a trail through the sugar bush, when a hen grouse came fluttering out of the ferns and ran off dragging a wing behind her, cheeping loudly to divert our attention from her brood of half-grown chicks.

We're moving to Vermont.

We'll be there in time for Will to start school next fall.

~

It's the last Saturday in November and the final day of the early small game season. On this cool and breezy day, traces of snow lie on the ground and clouds chase across a deep blue sky. The mountains are purple gray. In the clear air, every hill and hollow, every woodlot and farm field, stand out sharply.

I drive to Burnt Baker. After parking at the usual pullout, I turn Caillie loose and load the gun. I look up at the steep slopes that cradle the best part of the covert. It's possible that I will run into another grouse hunter up there today, although it seems more likely that I will encounter deer hunters scouting out places to sit this coming Monday, when the two-week deer season opens. (Tomorrow, Sunday, I'll be doing some scouting of my own: I pick up two more vacation days in December, and I plan to use one for the Monday opener.)

Caillie splashes through the stream, and I ford it on a couple of rocks. The brook is running full. It's good to see such a healthy flow after all the drought years.

Caillie swings out beyond the first patch of cover, turns, and comes zigzagging back. Her body low, she shoulders through the brush. She hunts with her nose down and keeps within gun range. As we get farther into the covert, I find to my satisfaction that I do not have to use the whistle much.

The deciduous trees are bare, except for some of the oaks, which still clasp a few dry brown leaves. Tufts of broomsedge in the fields are a warm orangey gold; backlit by the sun and pushed to and fro by the wind, they flicker like flames. In the woods, the duff underfoot is a dull brown with only a few flecks of color remaining on the fallen leaves.

Caillie works along on the downwind side of a blowdown. Branch stubs hold the broken trunk a foot off the ground. Dead leaves still attached to the fallen tree's twigs make a soft rasping in the wind. As I have done so many times this fall, I stare at this hospitable fragment of grouse cover and will a bird to flush from it. But no bird is in residence.

We keep on moving through the covert. I watch Caillie and try to think a few steps ahead of her. I try to orchestrate our combined movements so that I'm never boxed in by the brush, so that I can be facing toward the places where she's hunting. We check out all of the likely spots. I have paused among some sumacs and old stumps when a grouse flushes: it's out of sight, somewhere up the slope. I change course and hunt toward the flush. Ten minutes later, I hear the bird flush again. This time I glimpse the grouse, but with so many crisscrossed branches in the way, there is no shot.

It's not surprising that the birds are wild again today in the wind. And they are so few that I fully understand their evasiveness.

We keep on hunting in the general direction the grouse has flown. We hunt for a long way, and we do not flush the grouse a third time.

We make another big sweep, this one including a thicket of mountain laurel several acres in extent. The shrubs' slick leaves flash in the sunlight.

No grouse.

I slow down and take in my surroundings. The way the differently shaped leaves lie upon the earth, seeming to intermesh like the parts of a puzzle. A patch of dirt where a buck, goaded by the rut, scraped with his hoof beneath a witch hazel; he also used his antlers to break off some branches on the bush. A brown creeper—a tiny dark bird with a downward-curving bill—preens the ridged bark of a chestnut oak, hunting for spiders and insects. Frost-killed ferns lie on the ground like dirty discarded lace.

Almost everywhere I hunt at Burnt Baker, I come upon grape tangles. The thick, resilient vines lie in dark loops and coils on the forest floor. They hang from the crowns of trees. While standing quietly during deer season, I have watched squirrels hauling huge mouthfuls of grapevine bark up into trees, there to stuff it inside cavities in the trunks: the shreddy bark insulates their nests. A grapevine will patiently climb a tree, inching higher year after year. A grapevine snaking across the forest floor may attach itself to a seedling, then ride it skyward as the seedling grows to become a tree. As the sun passes across the sky, the leaves of a grapevine move independently, pivoting to catch the sunlight filtering down through the forest canopy.

This has not been a good year for grapes, and in Burnt Baker only a few clusters of the fruit, now dark and shriveled, hang from the vines. Wild animals love to eat grapes: bears, skunks, foxes, and raccoons. Sometimes the creatures leave their droppings, filled with seeds, at the bases of trees; the grapevines sprouting there find a ladder close at hand. A host of birds feed on the fruit, including woodpeckers, turkeys, cedar waxwings, cardinals, catbirds, and all of the woodland thrushes. I have killed many grouse whose crops were stuffed with the tart purple fruits. And grouse love to hide in grape tangles, where the vines, having grown weighty, have broken free from their tree supports and now lie coiled and asprawl on the ground.

We hunt until dusk, and I don't see another soul in Burnt Baker. Caillie and I move four grouse a total of six times. I end up not firing a shot.

Chapter 16

After the solstice, life turns in on itself. Toads and frogs and snakes and salamanders lie tucked away in the leaf litter, buried inside rotten logs, embracing the muck at the bottoms of ponds. Their hearts slowly tick away the cold. The migratory birds have fled, gone on long and miraculous journeys. The birds that remain in our northern latitudes perform their own miracles by surviving from one day to the next. The colors these birds wear are mainly subdued ones. The ministerial black of ravens and crows. Woodpeckers, nuthatches, and chickadees in businesslike gray and black and white. The occasional cardinal that visits our feeder shines like a beacon; a blue jay is a shard of sky brought to earth. If you look closely, some of the drab species show startling colors: blood red at the nape of a downy woodpecker's neck, gold on a kinglet's crown. Grouse wear a blanket of down beneath their cryptic plumage. If enough snow falls, the grouse will burrow into it at night. Under the snow, in what is known as the subnivean environment, the temperature can be fifty degrees warmer than the air above.

The deer have long since shed their ruddy summer pelage and replaced it with a slaty gray brown: the thick, insulating "blue coat" that hunters refer to. I had good luck with the deer this year. On the first day of the season I shot the biggest buck I have ever taken. He had four points on each antler beam, and the spread between his beams was almost twenty inches. He was a heavy animal, and it was hard work dragging him on bare ground and getting him into the truck. Then on the first Saturday of the season, not far from where I'd killed the buck, I shot a young male deer, a fawn this past spring. His meat is exceptionally tasty and tender.

On Christmas, it snowed ten inches. We spent a quiet day celebrating our last Yule at Mountain Road. In the afternoon, Nancy and I went out on cross-country skis. That night the wind rose and blew the snow all around, and in the morning I had to clear off our lane again. The university closes between Christmas and New Year's, so I'm on break from my job. Right now, the late small-game season is open. On the day after Christmas, I worked on my writing in the morning. After lunch, I planned to get out for grouse.

~

At first I can't decide where to hunt. With this much snow, just walking on level ground will be hard work, and a steep mountain slope could be treacherous. I consider those of my coverts that are flat (there aren't many) or at least gentle. I could go to Pufferbelly, but I don't want to listen to the highway noise. Everyman's, but I'd have to put up with traffic racket there, too. The Jay Place? Probably the landowner will be out hunting today, and I wouldn't want to get in his way. When Nancy and I were skiing yesterday, we cut some grouse tracks on Black Oak Ridge. The tracks headed toward a brushy slope on the far side. It's hilly ground, but the area is laced with logging roads that ought to make it fairly easy to get around. I used to hunt several small coverts on the far side of the ridge, but I haven't visited them in years.

Caillie and I trudge through our pasture. The horses watch us. Insulated as fully as any deer, they're covered with ice and snow and are much happier being out in the weather than standing around in a barn. In the woods beyond the pasture, deer tracks stitch the snow. Over the years, I have killed many whitetails on our land—now I'm reluctant to shoot my rifle here, what with all of the houses that have gone up in the vicinity. When we first built, I did a lot of hunting in the surrounding cutover land, both for deer and for grouse. There's something especially satisfying about being able to hunt right off your doorstep.

The late grouse season is a spare and elemental time of the year. It's usually cold enough that I can climb the hills and cover the miles without overheating. I wear a wool shirt beneath my gunning vest, and my deer hunting boots with the cleated soles. Cutting through our woods, I'm cold at first, but as I hike toward Black Oak Ridge I get warmed up; even my hands, clad in thin deerskin gloves, are comfortable. I follow along next to our yesterday's ski trail, which the blowing snow has almost erased. At the ridgetop I turn onto a logging road that angles down the far slope. It's slippery going. I skid and stumble. Leaning back for safety, I fall on my rear end twice. One of those times I plug the ends of my gun barrels with snow, and must open and unload the shotgun and blow through the barrels to clear them.

Below me, a pileated woodpecker loops between the trees in its irregular, dipping flight. With its great wingspan and its strongly crested head, the bird looks like a pterodactyl. It swoops up to a chestnut oak, pivots in midair, and lands on the side of the trunk, clamping itself in place like a refrigerator magnet. It's as big as a crow, with a solid black back and a black-and-white head topped with a red crest. Pileated woodpeckers eat a lot of carpenter ants: I've watched the big birds whacking their bills into trees to excavate ant colonies, and they can really make the chips fly. I knew an old woman who referred to the pileated as "Lord God Woodpecker"; she wanted in the worst way to shoot one, so that she could get a closer look at it. This pileated on Black Oak Ridge is in no danger of being shot. When the bird sees me, it lets go of the trunk and flies off, its crazy laughter ringing through the woods.

Near the bottom of the slope, another logging road branches off and runs along on the level. I turn onto it. On my left, the land continues down more gently, with a band of trees about seventy-five yards wide lying between the logging track and some farm fields. I walk west along the road, into a breeze. Up to her belly in the snow, Caillie can't help but keep close. She explores the patches of cover on either side of the road. She sniffs around some blackberry canes arching over a snowcapped log. She plows through a tangle of grapevines and multiflora rose. We check a stand of sumac, with its antlerlike branches and fuzzy twigs: the upright red seedheads identify the shrub as a female. Songbirds often eat sumac seeds, and sometimes grouse do, too. Beneath the shrub, a few stray seeds and some reddish fuzz lie on the snow. Something—it must have been a bird, since there are no tracks beneath the shrub—has been working on the sumac since yesterday's snowfall.

I'm standing with my eye on the dog when a grouse flushes. Caillie wasn't working the bird, which comes up behind us and about thirty yards up the slope. It flies back over the hill that we have just struggled down. I consider the possibility that this could be the only grouse we encounter today, and for a moment—but only for a moment—I think about turning around and climbing after it.

Out in front, the cover looks pretty decent, albeit with more multiflora rose than I remembered: the wicked stuff has been spreading. I hie Caillie on. I keep to the logging road and direct the spaniel through the best of the cover where it spreads uphill. We push forward for a hundred yards, then another hundred.

The road leads us into a big area overgrown with rose. Sometimes I can see Caillie, and sometimes she's hidden among the thorns. She picks her way forward to a small opening, where she stops and sticks her nose into the snow. Her tail speeds up. She takes a couple of snow-kicking bounds, sniffs frantically, bounds again. Quickly I find myself an opening.

The eternal dilemma when hunting behind a flushing dog: stay where you are and be ready, or try to get closer for a possible shot? I keep my feet planted. The cover is dense from about head level down, but relatively open above that, with scattered locust, maple, and birch trees. If Caillie roots a grouse out of this patch, and if it flushes within thirty yards of where I'm standing, I ought to have a shot.

A bird catapults up from the snow. It flies downhill. I time my swing so that the moment the grouse crosses the logging road, the shotgun's buttstock finds my shoulder. The 20 gauge barks, and the grouse tumbles down into snow-bedecked thorns. I hear its wings beating, a rapid thudding that gradually slows and stops. Caillie pushes her way into the thicket. When she finally finds the bird, she picks it up and selects a return route, moving toward me—I give the whistle a few quiet pips—until it's too thick and thorny, whereupon she backtracks and tries another route. I have to infer much of this sequence, because, other than an occasional glimpse, I can't see my dog. After almost five minutes, Caillie emerges from the tangle with the grouse in her mouth.

She delivers the bird to me. The grouse looks like it has been through the wringer. Caillie didn't mangle it, but the thornbushes certainly did. The grouse is lacking all but one tailfeather. Its neck is bereft of feathers— the pasty, goose-bumped flesh is as naked as that of a supermarket fowl. Other than missing a considerable percentage of its plumage, the bird appears to be sound: no tooth marks, torn skin, or broken bones.

I give Caillie a pat on the head. "Good girl," I tell her. "You're a good dog."

~

Through the rest of the Christmas break, I am able to make it out hunting three times.

One afternoon I get out during a snowfall. Snow covers every bush and branch in the covert I call Porky's. In the white and gray landscape, my orange vest and the spaniel's pink tongue are the only bright colors. The snow falls steadily, tiny white needles like metal filings. They trickle down my collar. The footing is poor, but a freezing rain earlier in the week has coated the thorns of the plentiful greenbrier and rose, and I can grab onto the shrubs, as well as the saplings that grow here densely, when I need to hold myself in place on the slope. Our route through the covert intersects a fresh trough in the snow: I am just as happy not to have met with the trough's maker, and the covert's namesake, since Caillie has been incautious around porcupines in the past.

We hunt for almost two hours before we move a bird. We're almost back to the truck when Caillie flushes a grouse. It flies across the woods road in front of me, but it's too far out for a killing shot, and the last thing I want to do is to stick one pellet in a bird and doom it to a lingering death. We flush the bird again, in cover too thick for me to see it, let alone shoot at it. Caillie puts out another bird, and it, too, is just a bit too distant for me to feel comfortable with pulling the trigger.

A few days later, Dale and I visit Burnt Baker. In the hollow not far from the scorched foundation, I hear Dale's gun: two sudden reports, *bang-bang*. Later I learn he missed a grouse. Then the same thing, farther into the covert: *bang-bang*. When I get closer, I see Ginger finishing up her retrieve; Dale takes a grouse from her and puts it into his pouch. I ask him if he is developing a new wingshooting technique: shoot fast, twice, at every bird.

The hills gleam an icy blue gray, a shade paler than the slate gray clouds that lie in bands across the sky. We're hunting on six inches of new snow. I heard on the radio that places to the north and east of us got a couple of feet, which, had it fallen here, would have effectively ended our bird season.

I get one chance at a grouse, and it's a good one. A blowdown lies uphill from where I'm hunting, and I'm tired enough that I mentally ask myself if it's worth checking out. I decide that it is, and up the slope I go. Caillie labors along above the blowdown, then turns downhill. She dives among the fallen trees, and out comes a grouse. It flies toward me, then banks hard to the right, exposing the vulnerable breast and side. But I can't get the gun's safety off: my gloves are soaked from parting the snow-laden branches, from brushing snow off my pants after having fallen, and from pulling ice balls off the spaniel. I am reduced to standing and watching as the bird vanishes among the saplings. I remove my gloves and follow, but it's as if the snow-covered mountain has swallowed up the grouse.

On the last day of my Christmas break, I decide to try Frustration Covert, down the road from our house, for an hour at day's end. Sun and sky play their last light upon the hills, casting a far-off field in bluish purple, another area pink, another mauve, another a pale soft green. The trees' limbs are coated with snow. Irregularly shaped clumps of snow hang in the tops of the witch hazels. I find where a predator has taken a squirrel: a hank of coarse gray hair and a string of entrails lie in a roughly circular area beaten down in the snow, with the marks of wing pinions stitching the circle's outer edge. Probably a goshawk or a red-tailed hawk did the killing.

Not a grouse or a grouse track do I see. It's the second time this year I've hunted here—the first time was back in October—without moving any birds. I guess I can put this covert to bed for the year: I can put it to bed forever.

Chapter 17

On the last day of the extended grouse season, I head for a covert I haven't hunted in two years. I park near an old cemetery, in a clearing in the woods. In summer people put out small American flags in metal holders to decorate the graves of Civil War soldiers resting in this ground. When I first started hunting here, Henderson Cemetery lay by itself at the end of a rutted dirt road. Beyond it were three or four tumbledown cellar holes. Now, three new houses stand nearby, and the road has been graded level.

No Trespassing signs warn me away from a slope that used to be good for grouse. With Caillie at heel, I follow a logging road into the brushy woods to the left of the posted ground. The road curves around the side of a hill, descending and leaving the houses behind.

A mix of pale gray and dark gray clouds fill the sky. The massed clouds move slowly southward above the bluish, snow-dusted mountains. Zones of yellow and pink lie along the horizon. It's the middle of the afternoon, but already the colors of evening have begun to tint the sky.

When the road starts cutting through some likely looking cover, I release Caillie. Slate-colored juncos feed in the snow beneath a patch of weeds; at Caillie's approach, they flit up into the surrounding trees, their white outer tailfeathers flashing. We kick out a band of deer, six or eight of them; the deer keep moving ahead of us, not panicking, just staying far enough in front that I only catch a glimpse of them every now and then. A big bird flies out of a snag. It's a goshawk, with a blue-gray back and a pale breast; it goes coursing off through the woods with steady, powerful wing-beats. Goshawks are maneuverable enough to fly through the brush after a grouse, and willing to land and pursue their quarry on foot, running through the cover—although not on a powdery snow such as the one now covering the ground.

The logging road heads eastward, losing elevation as it goes. It passes among fallen oaks and heaps of logging slash, then near a dilapidated hunting camp. The camp is an old farmhouse; apparently someone tried to eke out a living by farming in this hollow years ago. The road wends on past a damp spot, where a few cattails stand above the snow. It nears an isolated stand of white pine, then cuts through patches of sumac and autumn olive and scattered greenbrier and grape tangles. Caillie and I check out all of these areas of potential grouse cover without seeing or hearing a bird flush.

As it descends, the hollow points toward the valley, beyond which rises Bald Eagle Ridge. Much of the time, I'm looking right across at Skytop, at the long scar, white with snow, that shows where the excavation for the interstate cuts through the ridge.

There's a tavern in State College with a lot of old photographs of Centre County hanging on the walls. One of the pictures shows Bald Eagle Valley, from the vantage point of Skytop. I'm not sure just when the photo was taken, but the road, Route 220, looks more like a country lane than a federal highway. The picture was made on a sunny summer day, with puffy white clouds casting their shadows on hayfields and houses and barns. The image shows many more farms, both on the valley floor and in the side hollows, than exist in the valley today. I have stood with a beer in my hand looking at that photograph for minutes on end, staring at the gently rolling landscape, trying to find my coverts. They aren't there. They have not yet emerged; they are all still sleeping beneath the farms.

Bald Eagle Valley. I'd like to call it my valley, but I don't know if I can or if I should. The folks who have lived here for generations, the descendants of the Civil War veterans and the other men and women buried at Henderson Cemetery, do not seem willing to acknowledge my claim on the land, I who have lived and hunted in this vale for only twenty years. Still, I think I understand their clannishness and their suspicion. People have lived poor in this valley for a long time, and in the shadow of that superior university, and it should come as no surprise that they want the money and the comforts they think they see coming. I believe they will end up in sorrow over what they ultimately will lose, but I guess I can't blame them for wanting that which they've never had.

I'm brought back to the present by a wind that comes blowing up the hollow, dislodging snow from the trees and making my eyes water.

Caillie is on my right. In front of her, some grapevines lie beneath the trees, further complicated by a spread of greenbrier. Caillie slows. Something about the look of the patch makes me slow, too, and stand straighter and stare at the cover a bit sharper and move the buttstock of the 20 gauge closer to my shoulder.

A grouse flushes. It angles toward the road. I swing the shotgun from right to left. The shot is almost an exact repeat of the one I took in killing the grouse on Black Oak Ridge a couple of weeks ago. The bird in its flight describes a symmetrical arc: up and out of the cover, killed at the top of its rise, and falling down gently into the snow.

I stand waiting in case another grouse flushes. But nothing further develops as Caillie gathers up the dead grouse and brings it to me.

It's a full-feathered, broad-tailed bird. A male, although not a particularly large one; likely he was hatched this past spring. My shot took him in the front end. Using my forefinger, I probe his crop: it's slack and empty.

In the rosy light I go and find where the grouse had been sitting, next to the barkless trunk of a fallen oak. The grouse had rested in that spot long enough to have defecated twice: a pair of curved olive-and-white droppings lie in a bowl-shaped depression in the snow. Faint lacy marks show where the grouse's outer wing feathers scratched the white surface when the bird flushed.

I follow the line of tracks backward. After thirty feet, I come to a hole in the powder about eight inches across and eight inches deep. The grouse left this snow bed in the morning. He didn't feed. He walked ahead for a short distance and settled in at the base of the downed oak. When Caillie and I came along, he was probably ready to get up and find food. He would have done so hastily in the twilight. Finished with his meal—grapes, greenbrier fruits, sumac seeds, aspen buds—he would have glided down to the ground and burrowed into the snow, there to spend the long winter night.

The day is fading fast. We turn and begin the long walk back to the cemetery. Working in the snow, Caillie has built up ice balls on the fur covering her chest and belly. The dangling balls of accreted snow and ice so encumber her that she ends up following in my tracks, at first a few feet behind me, then fifty feet, then a hundred. I turn and look back at her. I have to chuckle at the sight of my hard-charging, headstrong spaniel reduced to plodding along through the snow. I call to her, and she comes limping up to me. I unload the gun and lean it against a tree. I sit down in the snow, and pick up her feet one by one, and bite away the lumps that have built up on the fur between the pads. I break up and remove the balls that have accumulated between the tops of her legs and her torso. I can't get rid of all of the balls clogging up her undercarriage; the truck's heater will loosen them.

Darkness is approaching. The wind has died down. We continue on toward the cemetery.

~

Back home, in the gloaming I look for a chunk of pinkish sandstone lying in the tree strip between our house and the horse pasture. Left over after the building of our house, the stone marks my old spaniel's grave. It's covered with snow, but I find it and brush the snow from its top.

I don't like to leave this grave behind. (I must admit I am less remorseful about leaving my parents' graves: they chose to be cremated, and the memorial park where their remains are interred is just east of a shopping mall and across the street from a brand new convenience store and an interstate interchange.) It has been a year now since Jenny died. But she's present in my mind, tied to the many memories she helped me gather in the uplands. One of those memories shines brightly for me now. It happened on a day much like this one, at a place less than a mile from Henderson Cemetery in a covert we call Christmas Tree.

That moniker came about when Carl flushed a grouse out of a shrubby hemlock that stood by itself, like a Christmas tree, in the middle of some oak brush. I can't remember now if he connected on that long-ago bird— a shot like that one can be tough, since a grouse will often glide silently from a tree perch, without the loud wing-thuds that signal an off-the-ground flush.

On the day I'm remembering, half a foot of snow covered the ground. It was just Jenny and me. We worked our way through a patch of mountain laurel. Lines of grouse tracks wound between the twisted, springy stems; the tracks lay in troughs about two inches deep. I heard a grouse flush out of range. The bird seemed to be headed in the same direction in which we were moving—toward the Christmas tree.

We entered a maze where dead oaks had fallen one on top of the other. Briars surrounded the logs, and grapevines lay like snarled rusty cables on top of them. Red maples and witch hazels grew thickly all around.

Jenny dashed in under a witch hazel, her tail wagging furiously. I stood waiting for a flush, but it never came.

Grouse tracks pottered about between the bushes. Jenny sniffed all along the top of a log and jumped down on its far side. I expected a bird to erupt from the lee of the log, but that didn't happen, either. Clearly, Jenny was finding scent; maybe the birds had fed here a few hours earlier, and then had moved on.

A raven flew over, small and black against the firmament. Fox tracks— the prints arranged in a straight line—went through the cover. Chickadees flitted through the brush, calling softly to each other.

At the head of the hollow, I had two choices: turn right and hunt along a south-facing hillside with more fallen dead trees and sunny openings and grape tangles, or bear left and work toward the Christmas tree.

We set off along the south-facing slope. In one of the grape tangles, Jenny dived into one side of a blowdown, and a grouse flushed from the other side. I shot, and the grouse tumbled into the snow, rolling downhill for a few feet. Jenny was on it quickly. She hitched it up into her mouth, turned, and padded toward me.

It was a big bird. I knew it for a mature male from the breadth of its tail; later, I would measure the fan's spread at more than fourteen inches. But what really caught my eye was the grouse's coloring. Silvery gray flecked the plumage on its head, wings, and back. Instead of the usual chestnut-colored tail, the feathers showed alternating zones of tan, dark brown, and silver, broken near the tip by the customary black band. In my years of hunting grouse, I had taken only one other bird with silvery plumage.

We continued onward. Soon we reached the end of the series of grape tangles. We turned left and worked back along the top of the ridge, headed toward the lone hemlock—the Christmas tree.

I glimpsed the tree's deep green foliage in the distance. Years earlier, loggers had taken the mature oaks all around it. The hemlock wasn't a large tree: maybe twenty-five feet, no taller. Deer had browsed off the lower growth up to about five feet, but above that height the boughs were bushy and thick with needles. A grouse could hide in the tree and never be seen. A lot of grouse had done just that, and it always seemed to be my luck to approach the tree on the side opposite where the bird was sitting, so that I rarely got off a shot if a grouse happened to flush.

I hunted toward the hemlock one slow stride at a time, advancing with my left foot, then bringing up my right foot after it, ever ready to shoot. I tried to concentrate on what Jenny was up to, but I remained more aware of the locus of cover contained within the tree. Slipping through the brush and the laurel, I got to within twenty feet of the hemlock. As I was trying to decide which side of the tree to go around, I heard two wingbeats, followed by silence. I did the only thing I could think of: I went to my knees in the snow.

True to form, the grouse had flown out of the far side of the tree. It glided down almost to the level of the brush before flapping its wings again. I snapped off a shot. A few needles drifted down where the pattern had clipped the hemlock's lowest boughs. Jenny, too, had heard the grouse and had gone running toward it. I waited, kneeling in the snow. The sight picture had seemed right. But the bird had vanished into the brush as I'd shot, and I had no idea whether or not I had hit it.

Back came Jenny, weaving through the laurel, carrying the dead grouse. It was just as large and heavy as the silvery bird I had shot. Its tail, drooping, spread to an extraordinary breadth, and the bird's coloration was incredible. I had seen another such grouse; rather, I had seen a fan from a similar bird pinned to the wall at a friend's hunting camp.

The grouse had a coppery cast to its plumage. Where black would fret the feathering of a normal grouse, on this bird a metallic cinnamon gleamed. The tail band and shoulder ruffs shone like polished bronze.

I got the silvertail out and stood holding the two birds and looking at them for a long time. I put both birds back in my game pouch, where they gave good weight. The gun broken across my forearm, I turned and stared at the hemlock. It stood there silent and immobile. A little snow dressed its dark, filagreed crown.

It was a good time to be a hunter. The birds were there, and they were the heart and the soul of the land. I had a good dog. I had a valley full of coverts. I felt that I would go back to the Christmas tree again and again, for many years to come.

∼

It's cold in the tree strip. The lights are on in the house. I can smell smoke from the woodstove. Nancy is probably wondering what I'm doing, standing around in the dark.

I can barely make out Jenny's grave marker. I think about the overgrown family plots I've come upon when hunting for grouse, the frost-heaved headstones, the names they bear covered by lichens and effaced by years of rain. I think about the cramped cellar holes and the broken porcelain dolls and the fire-scorched rocks and the tumbledown barn foundations and the big rusted horseshoes and the dwindling lilac shrubs and the bushy leaning apple trees, and it is no solace, no solace at all, to come to an understanding that nothing lives forever, not even in memory: not the coverts we hunt, nor the birds we pursue, nor the dogs we hold close and whose bodies we memorize with our hands; nor the partners who accompany us on our days afield; nor the loved ones with whom we share our lives; nor parents, nor wives, nor sons, nor daughters, nor ourselves.

But I don't know what else to do, other than to keep on living life, keep on savoring life. The way to live it to the fullest is to do the things that make your heart sing. To love well a wife and a child, to remember parents who loved you just as dearly, to gallop a horse down a sand road, to put your nose behind a dog's ear and breathe in its smell, to climb high and hunt hard, to pursue wild birds that are doing their own level best to escape you.

$\mathcal{P}$ostscript

$\sim$

The Wild Branch flows swiftly between brown and tan rocks. It spreads out and glides more slowly past low sand-and-cobble stretches lined with aspens and alders. We're hunting among those fringing bands of trees, Dave, Winston, and I.

I am pleased at how quickly I have met fellow bird hunters in Vermont—and at how generously they have shared their coverts with me, in this, my first autumn in the north.

I've also hunted by myself in the old reverting fields around our house, among twinkling gold aspens, brilliant orange and yellow sugar maples, burnished tamaracks, and deep green spruces, cedars, and pines. Caillie and I have flushed woodcock in the low areas, and grouse in the hills.

Right now, there's a grouse weighing down my game pouch, a plump gray-phase male. Caillie flushed the grouse, which alighted for a moment in a tall aspen: as the bird launched himself from the branch, my shot tumbled him. I'm carrying my tried-and-true bramble divider, the Jeffery 20 gauge. I'm glad I made the shot, because I didn't get to practice with the gun very much over the summer, what with doing carpentry work. But the old house is nice and snug now, and two woodstoves are in place and six cords of hardwood lie stacked in the shed.

We're almost back to where we started working the covert. Apparently Dave and Winston have decided that the day's hunting is over: They're up on the bank to my left, behind a screen of trees, walking along on the edge of a hayfield, where I can hear their voices. I'm down next to the stream, keeping to the sandy areas where the going is quiet.

I catch a flash of white: Caillie slips through the alders just below the lip of the hayfield.

The grouse comes hurtling out of the low trees. Seeing me, it banks to its left and heads across the creek. My shot catches it when it's directly above the Wild Branch. The bird's head falls and its wings tuck back against its sides and its momentum carries it across the water. The grouse falls in the grass on the far side.

Caillie emerges from the alders. She runs over to me. I sit her down with a pip on the whistle. I put my hand in front of her nose, with my fingers pointed toward the fallen grouse. I move my hand like an arrow in the direction of the fall.

I release her: "Caillie!"

She wades into the creek and starts swimming. The line I gave her puts her downwind of the grouse; as soon as she climbs onto the far bank, she turns into the wind, catches the scent, and dives into the grass. She picks up the bird, then turns and trots down to the Wild Branch and swims back across.

"Good girl," I tell her, as she comes out of the stream, the water dripping off her belly, darkening the rocks. Her eyes are on mine. She lays the grouse in my hand.